SEX

WEIRD

O

PEDIA

SEX WEIRD-O-PEDIA

The Ultimate Book of Shocking, Scandalous, and Incredibly Bizarre Sex Facts

ROSS BENES

Racehorse Publishing

Racehorse Publishing books may be purchased in bulk at special discounts for sales promotion, corporate gifts, fund-raising, or educational purposes. Special editions can also be created to specifications. For details, contact the Special Sales Department, Skyhorse Publishing, 307 West 36th Street, 11th Floor, New York, NY 10018 or info@skyhorsepublishing.com.

Racehorse Publishing™ is a pending trademark of Skyhorse Publishing, Inc.®, a Delaware corporation.

Visit our website at www.skyhorsepublishing.com.

10 9 8 7 6 5 4 3 2 1

Library of Congress Cataloging-in-Publication Data is available on file.

Cover design by Daniel Brount

Print ISBN: 978-1-63158-437-4
Ebook ISBN: 978-1-63158-446-6

Printed in China

To Mom and Dad,
thanks for having sex so that I could exist.

contents

SEX

WEIRD

••• O •••

PEDIA

INTRODUCTION

Whether you are an abstinent virgin or a kinky horndog, one thing we can all agree on is that sex manifests itself throughout society in bizarre ways.

In this book, we are not focused on exalting or demonizing sex. Instead, we are just stating facts so that you can better appreciate the wonders of copulation. Some of the things sex affects include crime, how much money people save, and what we eat for breakfast. It is also something that nearly 10,000 Americans die in the act of each year. But no human has ever officially done it in outer space.

♥

The approach that municipalities take toward sex varies widely. Some US states ban the sale of sex toys but do not ban sex with dead people. Many countries prohibit prostitution, but in parts of Germany where there are not enough people to take care of the elderly, the state experimented with turning hookers into nurses. Meanwhile, several ancient societies around the world insisted that their top civil servants be castrated in an effort to stamp out nepotism.

♥

Primates like us do not have a monopoly on weird sex. Strange boning can be witnessed throughout the animal kingdom from water bugs that produce construction-zone levels of noise by rubbing their penis against their abdomen to sharks giving virgin births. And do not forget about the fish with flame-retardant sperm.

♥

Some of these facts sound too odd to be true. Sources (page 113) at the end of this book will point you in the right direction if you are looking to do some independent research, but if you start doing your own investigations, you may want to brace yourself. My legs have been crossed ever since I found out that sex research pioneer Alfred Kinsey shoved toothbrushes into his urethra.

CHAPTER 1
ANIMALS

Leopard slugs have penises that come out of their heads, and since they are hermaphroditic both slugs can bear offspring when a pair mate. According to limacologists (an amazing word used to describe scientists who study slugs), leopard slugs mate by hanging upside down and wrapping their gooey penises around each other in a "chandelier configuration."

Sea slugs have even stranger sex than their leopard brethren. After a sea slug mates, it discards its penis and grows another one within 24 hours. Starbucks is more considerate about wasting plastic straws than these slugs are about throwing away their dongs.

Ducks might look silly when they dunk their heads in a lake and show off their butts to pedestrians, but there is nothing lame about their dicks. A ruddy duck's penis can extend past 8 inches and is covered in spines. Meanwhile, human penises average about 6 inches in length and aren't equipped with much armor.

The clitoris of the female hyena extends up to 7 inches from its body.

> Male alligators have permanent boners that hide inside their bodies.

Researchers have found that some animals engage in activity akin to prostitution. Female penguins, who need stones to build their nests, trade sex for the rocks that male penguins provide them.

Water bugs are the loudest animal in the world relative to their size. The tiny critter reaches nearly 100 decibels when it rubs its penis against its abdomen. Basically, there is a rock concert going on whenever a water bug does the nasty.

Male giraffes will drink the pee of their female counterparts to determine if they are fertile or not.

Male giraffes will drink the pee of their female counterparts to determine if they are fertile or not.

The antechinus, an Australian marsupial, mates for 14 hours straight and will screw until it goes blind or dies.

♥

Labord's chameleons die after they bone.

♥

Female praying mantises are known to bite off and eat the heads of their male counterparts while they have sex. Once beheaded, the male's corpse continues to thrust. This coital snack gives the female energy to produce more eggs, which incentivizes the sexual cannibalism.

♥

Soapberry bugs can mate for 11 days straight.

♥

A honeybee's penis gets ripped off during sex.

♥

Moths can detect pheromones from a few miles away.

♥

Australian jewel beetles have been known to mate with brown beer bottles. Some beetles have died while trying to copulate with these alcohol containers.

♥

Female lobsters rely on urine to entice their mates. They engage in foreplay by stroking each other with their feet before they molt their shells during mating.

♥

Some herring have flame-retardant sperm.

Barnacles may have the most interesting penises in the animal kingdom. Their penises can stretch up to 8 times the length of their body, which is the equivalent of Patriots quarterback Tom Brady erecting a 50-foot schlong. And while many species have dicks that can change size, few can alter their shape. Researchers found that barnacles living in gentle waters have long and thin penises that are good for reach, while those in rough waters have short and wider penises that are better for holding off strong waves. The researchers then transported rough-water barnacles to calmer waters and vice versa and found that after getting moved around, the barnacles started adjusting their penis shape to better fit their environment.

> **Argentine lake ducks use their corkscrew penises like a lasso to pull in females that they're mating with who are trying to escape. Their 17-inch dicks are the longest bird boners ever observed.**

Female ducks have evolved elaborate vaginas to fend off unwelcome mating attempts from overeager males. For instance, some female ducks have vaginas that twist in the opposite direction of their male counterparts' corkscrew penises.

♥

Just 3 percent of bird species have penises. Ostriches and ducks have dicks, but eagles and penguins do not. Birds without penises transfer sperm from male to female via a "cloacal kiss."

♥

When birds get erections, their penises usually fill up with lymph fluid instead of blood.

♥

Kangaroos have 3 vaginas.

♥

A snake penis has 2 prongs.

♥

Female wildebeests ovulate faster when they hear male wildebeests' mating calls.

♥

Calvin Klein colognes have sex appeal to animals, too. Captive tigers and jaguars are attracted to the brand's "Obsession for Men" scent.

♥

Researchers in the 1960s tricked turkeys into having sex with turkey mannequins. The researchers then wanted to see how far these turkeys would go, so they reduced their turkey model to a head on a stick. And guess what? The turkeys still humped the severed head-on-a-stick. But turkeys aren't total savages. Though they tried banging a turkey head without a body, they weren't into humping a headless turkey corpse. Turkeys have standards, too.

In case you don't find crows ominous enough, you should know that they have orgies with crow corpses.

> Aside from crows, dolphins, whales, squirrels, toads, and lizards have been caught engaging in necrophilia.

Dolphin penises are usually erect.

A horny dolphin that humped some swimmers in France led a French town to ban swimming and diving on one of its beaches.

The Icelandic Phallogenic Museum has penises on display from nearly 300 different animal species, including Homo sapiens. One man wants to have his dong cut off during his lifetime so he can donate to the museum and visit his own penis on display in a pickle jar. He named the member he aspires to sever "Elmo."

♥

Female trapdoor spiders have a unique way of showing that they are ready to get it on. Once the female spider is ready to mate, she spins a silk mat soaked with pheromones to attract suitors. And here you thought buying flowers was a chore.

♥

Yellow armadillos have sex while they're running. Talk about multitasking.

♥

Female prairie voles get turned on by their partners' urine.

♥

Rabbits are into water sports and will sometimes urinate on their partner before mating.

♥

You think your dry spell is long? You have got nothing on worms. After sequencing the DNA of asexual translucent worms, researchers discovered that one species had not had sex for over 18 million years.

♥

Female rodents will miscarry their pregnancy if they detect pheromones from unfamiliar males.

♥

Astronauts have artificially inseminated frog eggs in a space shuttle in orbit.

> **The first pregnant mammals to fly in outer space aboard a US spacecraft were rats.**

From peppers to oysters, humans have paired all sorts of meals with sex to arouse their partner. Animals indulge in aphrodisiacs, too. In one type of cricket, males produce a jelly when they ejaculate, and the female eats the jelly when the male's sperm enters her body. It is like combining sex and dinner without having to clean up afterward.

♥

As long as women have been on Earth, guys have done incredibly stupid things to try to impress them. It turns out that birds are not immune to this dynamic. Little birds like chickadees will group together to take on larger predators. It has generally been assumed that they do this for protection purposes, but researchers in Brazil came to a different conclusion. The researchers created a few fake owls, one from a species that regularly eats smaller birds and another from a less threatening owl species. They found that across 79 different species of small birds, the less threatening owl was attacked more often by the smaller birds. The conclusion was that the small birds used the weaker opponent as an opportunity to showcase their defense skills to potential mates.

♥

There really are apps for everything, including a few that will track your dog's menstrual cycles.

♥

In an effort to better understand how reproduction works in the absence of gravity, Russia's space agency launched 5 geckos into orbit in 2014 so that they could observe how the lizards boned in space. Sadly, the geckos froze to death before they touched back down to Earth.

> Australian scientists claim to have found a shark that gives "virgin births." They studied a female zebra shark named Leonie who laid eggs despite not being around a male shark in 3 years. Several years before her virgin birth, Leonie gave birth after mating with a male shark. She is believed to be the first known shark to reproduce both sexually and asexually.

In 2015, a brownbanded bamboo shark gave birth a few years after it had been inseminated by a male shark. Unlike Leonie, the virgin birth shark that shared no genetic link to any male shark, this bamboo shark had some DNA from the male shark who impregnated her. This shows that animal sperm can sometimes be stored for long durations while keeping its chemical makeup intact. Kind of like Twinkies.

♥

Male deep-sea anglerfish are pretty clingy. When anglerfish mate, the much smaller male bites into the tissue of the female and forms a permanent pair bond while slurping sustenance from her blood. The male anglerfish then just hangs out attached to his female partner until his body parts wither away and he becomes nothing more than a sperm donor riding her coattails. They're like the deep-sea version of Kevin Federline.

♥

Guppies take sperm storage to another level. Female guppies tend to outlive their male counterparts, and they've evolved to store sperm from multiple males simultaneously. In one study of wild guppies in Trinidad and Tobago, 1 in 4 were fathered by the sperm of dead males.

> Male bats are more likely to have large brains if their testicles are small.

A group of researchers found that fish become hornier when their water supply is contaminated by drugs like Prozac.

♥

Filmmakers use animal mating sounds to capture people's attention. For instance, some of the dinosaur sounds in *Jurassic Park* are actually recordings of tortoises getting it on.

CHAPTER 2
COMMERCIAL PRODUCTS

Forget those Axe commercials where women pounce on men who douse themselves with scented body spray. According to one study, men's cologne turns women off and reduces blood flow to the vagina.

During the Middle Ages in Europe, weasel nuts were used as a form of contraception. The belief was that tying weasel testicles around a woman's thigh or neck would prevent her from getting pregnant during sex.

Casanova used a pulped lemon as a contraceptive.

An app called Morning Glory helps men track how often they get boners.

♥

Italian fashion company Fendi sells a $986 scarf that looks like a vulva. People who wear the product and poke their heads through their scarf appear as if they are being born.

♥

A tableware and cutlery juggernaut started out as a hippie commune with lots of open sex. Oneida, now known for its silverware, began as a utopian community in upstate New York in the mid-1800s where members shared everything, including their spouses.

♥

In case you are desperate for a vibrator but not near a sex toy shop, you can always download an app that makes your phone repeatedly vibrate. If you decide to turn your phone into a sex toy, you may want to cover it and disinfect it.

> There are books full of recipes for cooking and making alcoholic drinks with human semen.

An entrepreneur plans to open up a cafe in London where a cup of coffee can be ordered alongside some oral sex that is given by a robot.

♥

The Internet of Things has brought us internet-connected wristwatches, fridges, and thermostats. It has also brought us internet-connected sex toys. Unfortunately, hackers can locate Bluetooth-powered butt plugs and control them from anywhere. Actually, that unfortunately was presumptuous on my part. Maybe that is something you are into.

♥

Clorox, the cleaning supplies and bleach brand, created an app called Sock-It that allowed horny college students to send a notification to their roommates signaling that roomies should leave before things get freaky. The app is named after the sock-on-the-doorknob trick that signals that the people inside the room are banging. It appears that Clorox did not win any marketing awards for this gimmick.

♥

Cock rings used to be made out of goat eyelids.

♥

The actor who played the purple dinosaur Barney on one of the most popular children's TV shows during the 1990s now runs a tantric sex business.

♥

Gwyneth Paltrow's lifestyle brand Goop paid $145,000 to settle a lawsuit about unscientific claims it made regarding the benefits of a $66 jade egg that supposedly increased sexual desire, regulated menstruation, and enhanced bladder control once it was inserted into a vagina.

♥

Just as Wonderbras make boobs look bigger, the Lee Cooper clothing company designed "Packit" jeans to make men's bulges stick out.

♥

Strip club owners have used clever tricks to get past city ordinances designed to ban them. A strip club in Eureka, California, rebranded itself as a recreational-vehicle promotion center by handing out brochures for RVs while women stripped. A titty bar in Ladson, South Carolina, converted itself into the "Church of the Fuzzy Bunny's [sic]," which featured pastors reciting Bible verses as dancers jiggled their breasts at patrons. And just outside of Orlando, Florida, a strip club took advantage of a loophole that allowed nudity in "bona fide performances" by having its dancers perform Shakespeare's *Macbeth* in the buff.

♥

After Alfred Kinsey's sex research reports became famous, all sorts of people ranging from fashion designers to novelists borrowed off the notoriety for their shameless marketing. A book of poems by a psychiatrist titled *Clinical Sonnets* was advertised as the "Kinsey report in verse."

> In 1946 Walt Disney animated a film for Kotex about menstruation.

Menstrual products couldn't be advertised on television in America until 1972, and they used to be sold behind the counter. The prudishness with which the United States has approached women's menstruation is still in effect today as some states still tax tampons even though they do not tax products aimed at men such as Viagra.

Men's cluelessness about menstruation was demonstrated when Sally Ride became the first American woman to enter outer space. Prior to Ride's weeklong journey in space, NASA engineers asked her if 100 tampons would be enough for the trip. (Closer to 20 tampons are used in a typical cycle.)

During the 1990s, a New York City retailer created a company called Time of the Month Inc. that sold novelty snacks such as PMS Crunch.

Online marketplaces sell tampons made out of bamboo.

Wilhelm Reich has been called the godfather of the "free love" movement and the originator of terms like "sex negative" and "sex positive," which stemmed from his open attitude toward sexuality. He developed boxes to contain a hypothetical life force he dubbed "orgone." These orgone boxes gained popularity especially among countercultural figures including J. D. Salinger, Norman Mailer, and Jack Kerouac, all of whom endorsed Reich. The term "orgone" came from the words "orgasm" and "organism" and was what others referred to as God, Reich said. To the normal person, orgone boxes looked like large empty closets, but to a devotee of orgone theory, these pseudoscientific contraptions could heal disease by leveling out the body's orgone levels. Woody Allen, a man with his own sexual neuroses no doubt, spoofed the product in one of his movies and called it the "Orgasmatron."

♥

Contraception is basically as old as human civilization. For centuries, women placed leaves, fruit, and in some cases, crocodile feces in their vaginas to avoid getting pregnant. Some scholars argue that animals have long relied on contraception too, including chimpanzees, who chew leaves containing contraceptive chemicals.

> Aristotle suggested cedar oil and olive oil can work as contraceptives if they are rubbed against a woman's cervix prior to sexual intercourse.

Margaret Sanger lobbied for the birth control pill because she wanted poorer people to have fewer children. Sanger said, "Birth control is nothing more or less than the facilitation of the process of weeding out the unfit, or preventing the birth of defectives or of those who will become defectives." Results have been opposite of what she intended, as the pill is used much more by the rich and middle class than it is by the poor.

♥

Bikini swimsuits get their name from the atomic bomb testing that took place at Bikini Atoll during the mid-twentieth century. The French designer who created the bikini chose that name as a marketing tactic, hoping his new product would shock people as much as A-bombs did.

> One fad among wine snobs is a preference for "natural wines" that are grown without preservatives and rely on manure for fertilizer. A sommelier at a high-end restaurant in New York City told a reporter that the horse-poop smell in the wine "triggers some sexual stuff. And I'm sure about that."

Whenever people wake up and chow down on some cereal, they indulge preachers' fantasies that milk and grain in the morning will curb masturbation. John Harvey Kellogg was a prominent Seventh-Day Adventist who edited books with his wife during his honeymoon in lieu of consummating his marriage and believed that children who masturbate should have carbolic acid poured on their genitals. Kellogg invented cornflakes with the premise that they would reduce libidinal urges. "The reproductive act is the most exhausting of all vital acts," Kellogg wrote. "Its effect upon the undeveloped person is to retard growth, weaken the constitution, and dwarf the intellect."

♥

The inventor of graham crackers also really hated sex. Sylvester Graham was a preacher who believed that diet had a huge impact on people's sex drives, so he invented the bland vegetarian food graham crackers in order to reduce the sinister urge. Graham thought sex should be avoided even within marriage.

♥

During the Victorian era, irritable women were diagnosed with a bogus catchall disease called "hysteria." And since masturbation was frowned upon, woman sought treatment for this "disease" from doctors who manually massaged their vaginas under the impression that the relief this provided would rid women of hysteria.

♥

Because these massages would take a painstaking hour, doctors invented the vibrator to speed up the process. "The funny thing is that the vibrator was kind of invented for a guy as a laborsaving device," said Tanya Wexler, director of *Hysteria*, a movie about the invention of the vibrator.

♥

Treatments for hysteria included spraying water into vaginas, dancing, and horseback riding. Galloping on horses may seem like a strange way to treat a sexually related condition, but it was not without precedent. Sexologists have reported patients getting aroused by riding horses and, in the 19th century, riding horses was used as an impotence treatment by some doctors.

♥

The Hitachi Magic Wand is still one of the most popular sex toys on the market nearly 50 years after it debuted even though its parent company markets it as a personal massager in an effort to distance the product from its commonplace use of getting women off.

> **Dildos and vibrators have led to police investigations and evacuations at airports in Thailand, Sudan, Australia, and Germany because authorities mistook the sex toys for bombs.**

> Viagra came about as an accident. Pfizer researchers were testing out a blood-pressure medication and noticed that patients kept wanting to take the drug home with them. This was because this test drug was giving patients raging boners, so Pfizer pivoted its marketing pitch, and Viagra was born. Viagra is obviously primarily used for sexual performance, but doctors still use the drug to treat various heart and lung conditions.

At an American Urology Association conference in Las Vegas in 1983, 57-year-old physiologist Giles Brindley brought attention to impotence research by exhibiting that old age wasn't preventing him from getting it up. For his research presentation, he was to demonstrate the effectiveness of injectable drugs in treating impotence, so he did what any middle-aged doctor would do. He injected the drug into his dong, commanded the stage, threw off his pants, and proudly showed off his erect penis. "I was wondering why this very smart man was giving his talk in a jogging outfit," a conference attendee told *Fortune.* "Then he stepped from behind the podium. It was a big penis, and he just walked around the stage showing it off."

Other doctors have tested sex drugs on themselves. One endocrinologist developing a drug that would tan skin while causing erections made a miscalculation when trying the product out on himself. He said: "I didn't develop a suntan right way, but I did develop an erection very rapidly. I developed an erection that lasted 8 hours. . . . I couldn't reduce it with ice cubes. I reached up and said, 'We're going to be very rich!'"

There are several things that can prevent a man from getting his dick up. But if the issue is psychological, then the man will still get an erection in his sleep. One way doctors have tested for nocturnal erections is by wrapping a roll of postage stamps around a patient's penis. If an erection did occur at night, doctors would theoretically be able to tell because the penis would bust through the perforations that connect the stamps. But if the perforations remained intact, either the man did not get an erection or he was unable to fuck his way out of a roll of stamps.

♥

In Egypt, Viagra is used as an alternative currency by some people. According to journalist Shereen El Feki: "I know of one man who carries a pocketful of the real thing, picked up in America, for baksheesh; the pills are especially useful, he says, for bribing bureaucrats to finish paperwork on time."

> For many years, insurance companies covered Viagra but not birth control pills.

Before Viagra became popular, vacuum pumps and penile surgeries were used to treat impotence. These procedures were more about cosmetics than functionality.

♥

Some scholars believe that sex toys have been around for at least 30,000 years.

♥

A ventriloquist who used the stage name Ted Marche went on to become a trailblazer in the strap-on dildo business. The operation was a family business as Marche's spouse and children pitched in to help design and sell the products.

♥

Alabama bans the sale of sex toys, but the state law has a loop-hole that allows people to sell sex toys as long as they are used for "medical, scientific, educational, legislative, judicial, or law enforcement" purposes. An ambitious sex toy shop called Pleasures took advantage of the loophole by having its customers fill out a questionnaire about their sexual difficulties. As long as someone reports a medical or scientific issue with their sex life, then they are fair game to become sex toy customers of the store. Another thing that makes the Pleasures store unique is that it operates out of an old bank building, which allowed it to repurpose the bank teller drive-thru window. The result is that Alabama folks can zip on through and order their dildos on the go as if they were picking up fast-food hamburgers.

CHAPTER 3
SCIENCE

Sex might seem strenuous when things get hot and heavy, but it usually is not that great of a workout. You have to hump for nearly 200 minutes to burn as much energy as you do during a 30-minute run. Mowing the lawn burns significantly more calories than sex. According to the British Heart Foundation, sex burns about the same amount of energy per minute as ironing clothes. Now how about a cigarette to bask in the glow of that wrinkle-free shirt?

In a study of several thousand pregnant women in the US, about 1 percent of the participants claimed they were virgins when they gave birth.

Men's testicles often differ in size and one hangs lower than the other. Usually it is the left nut that droops a little more.

Russian researcher Ivan Pavlov is famous for conditioning a dog to salivate at the sound of a bell. One of Pavlov's associates, W. Horsley Gantt, conditioned dogs to get erections and ejaculate when they hear specific tones.

According to the Smell and Taste Treatment and Research Foundation, blood flow to men's penises increases by 40 percent when they smell pumpkin pie and lavender.

♥

Most of the clitoris lies within a woman's body. It also has a shaft.

> It is possible for fraternal twins to have two different fathers.

In 1998, a group of US pharmacologists won a Nobel Prize for their work with the gas nitric oxide, which is used to widen blood vessels and give men erections.

♥

The pioneering sex researcher Richard von Krafft-Ebing didn't want his knowledge in the hands of ordinary folk, so he wrote the founding document of modern sexology, *Psychopathia Sexualis*, in Latin to discourage regular Joes from reading it.

♥

The practice of erotic asphyxiation—choking someone with the intention that cutting off oxygen to their brain will get them sexually aroused—is believed to have originated as a treatment for impotence.

♥

The renowned philosopher René Descartes had a thing for cross-eyed ladies.

♥

The pioneering scientist Albert Einstein married his first cousin.

> Greek philosopher Anaxagoras taught that semen from the left testicle produces girls while semen from the right testicle produces boys.

An 18th-century French anatomist advised his patients that a couple is more likely to bear a son if the father cuts off his left testicle.

♥

Charles Darwin, whose pioneering theories on evolution changed the way scientists approached many subjects including sexuality and reproduction, married his first cousin.

♥

Havelock Ellis, the coauthor of the first medical textbook in English on homosexuality, was impotent for most of his life, yet became aroused by women expelling their "liquid gold." Ellis believed fetishes began in childhood, and recalls a memory of his mom squatting to pee in some bushes at the zoo gardens, and how the sound of her urine hitting the ground excited him as a 12-year-old. He said, "I may be regarded as a pioneer in the recognition of the beauty of the natural act in women when carried out in the erect attitude."

♥

Kinsey's famous anthologies changed America's view on sex forever, but his research methods like his sampling techniques and reliance on self-reported data were shoddy by middle-school standards, so Kinsey's findings should be interpreted with many grains of salt. However, some of his conclusions are quite thought provoking, like the finding that the average penis length of gay men is 0.3 inches longer than the average penis length of straight men.

♥

In case you need evidence that social scientists prefer to talk like androids instead of speaking like actual human beings, the terminology that academics use to describe someone's first sexual experience has changed from "losing virginity" to "coitus" to "first sex" to "sexual debut."

Anxiety can boost sexual attraction. In one academic study, male participants walked over a suspension bridge and were then immediately approached by a female who offered her number. Some of the guys walked over a shaky bridge while those in the control group walked over a stable bridge. Those who walked over the shaky bridge mistook their fear for sexual arousal and were much more likely to ask the woman out on a date.

> Some doctors believe that orgasms can relieve sinus pressure.

Blood vessels in the genitals become engorged while people dream.

♥

Irrational sexual behaviors—like having unprotected sex with a stranger in an era where STDs are rampant or young people having their own children before they can financially support offspring—appear bewildering. But unreasonable sex may have benefited humans in the past. Natural selection favors projecting genes into the future over the well-being of the individual, which is why people have been compelled to pass on "selfish genes" even when it is not in their best interest to do so. "If sex were an entirely rational process, the species would probably have died out long ago," wrote AIDS researcher Helen Epstein.

♥

According to NASA, no humans have ever had sex in space. A Russian astronaut bluntly addressed the lack of space sex during an interview with journalist Mary Roach. "My friend asks me, 'How are you making sex in space?' I say, 'By hand!'"

♥

In what was not an April Fool's Day joke, NASA scientists began a mission on April 1, 2018, that involved sending human and bull sperm to outer space. Their intention was to study how microgravity affects the motility of sperm cells, because if humans are to ever colonize space, we must boldly study where no one has boned before.

> The first person to observe sperm cells was Antonie van Leeuwenhoek, who is considered by many to be the father of microbiology for the advancements he made to microscope technology and biology discoveries. After observing his own ejaculate, van Leewenhoek dubbed the tadpole-like cells he saw "animalcules."

Ovulation, when women are most likely to conceive, provokes differing responses from men and women. During this time, men take a stronger liking to women's natural odors. Women report a stronger desire to cheat and are less inclined to use a contraceptive during sex. Women also report that they wear more makeup, wear skimpier clothes, and feel more attractive during this stage of their cycle.

Premature ejaculation can be embarrassing as hell today, but according to psychologist Jesse Bering, it may have provided evolutionary advantages for ancient humans since it made it easier for males to inseminate many females in a shorter amount of time.

Research from evolutionary psychologists indicates that people's gender influences how they react to sexual jealousy. For men, they have a stronger reaction to sexual unfaithfulness than emotional infidelity. For women, it is the reverse. The theory behind these behaviors comes back to evolution. Males who were intolerant about their wives becoming sexually active with other men were less likely to become a cuckold and more likely to see their own genes pass onto future generations. Women who prevented their husbands from emotionally bonding with other females reduced the chances of their men spending their resources on other women.

Genetics may influence how likely you are to cheat on your significant other. Scientists at Binghamton University found people who had a particular gene were more likely to have a history of infidelity. Having or lacking this gene doesn't cause someone to cheat, but it can make them more inclined to do so, the scientists concluded.

> In a study called "The Coital Coronary," researchers estimated that just over 10,000 Americans die during sex per year.

In the 1960s, a NASA-funded research project led to some human-on-dolphin action. The male dolphin being observed was supposed to be transported to a pool with female dolphins whenever the dolphins became sexually aroused, but transporting dolphins is a logistical headache, so one of the human researchers just masturbated the male dolphin instead. "I wasn't uncomfortable with it, as long as it wasn't rough," the researcher said. "It would just become part of what was going on, like an itch—just get rid of it, scratch it, and move on. And that's how it seemed to work out. It wasn't private. People could observe it."

CHAPTER 4
STDS

Several STDs are rising among elderly people. Among people aged 55 and older in the United States, chlamydia has doubled, and gonorrhea has tripled since 2010.

♥

The go-to treatment for many STDs has been penicillin, but this drug was not intentionally created. Scottish scientist Alexander Fleming noticed weird fungus growing in one of his unclean petri dishes in 1928 and he found it interesting that the fungus killed bacteria. This fungus later became known as penicillin. By forgetting to clean the dishes, Fleming gave people with the clap reason to rejoice.

♥

Penicillin ain't as good as it once was. To the chagrin of doctors and their patients, the overuse of antibiotics has led microbes to develop resistance to antibiotics. Because of this trend, public health officials are worried that gonorrhea will lose its status as a curable sexual disease. The number of gonorrhea infections that are untreatable by antibiotics continues to rise.

> One economist says that penicillin, and not the birth control pill, was the real enabler of the sexual revolution. The study published in *Archives of Sexual Behavior* shows that penicillin contributed to a 75 percent decline in the number of deaths caused by syphilis from 1947 to 1957. Since the new treatment made sex safer, people started having riskier sex, which resulted in increases in the number of children born out of wedlock and teenagers getting knocked up.

Getting circumcised is one simple way a man can drastically reduce the probability that he will transmit HIV to his sexual partners. Because the foreskin of uncut penises is softer and thinner than the skin on the penis shaft, the foreskin tears easier during sex, which can let the HIV virus into the bloodstream. It is also moist under the foreskin, which allows viruses to survive. The World Health Organization claims that circumcision can reduce HIV risk by 60 percent.

After AIDS became an epidemic in several African countries, many of the world's largest drug companies eventually began selling their drugs at significantly reduced costs to AIDS-relief groups. Companies like to promote these initiatives to earn goodwill, but these changes came only after great resistance. When trying to get good PR, Bayer, Roche, GlaxoSmithKline like to leave out the part where they sued South Africa in the late 1990s after apartheid had ended because Nelson Mandela, South Africa's president at the time, had reduced drug prices for disease-stricken AIDS victims.

In the 1980s, the Castro regime in Cuba was aggressively testing its sexually active residents and sending people infected with the HIV virus to quarantined sanitariums. The government was also cracking down on social deviants by imprisoning them or forcing them into manual labor. To protect themselves from the intrusive policing, a group of Cuban punks intentionally infected themselves with HIV so that they would be quarantined rather than jailed since the sanitariums had superior accommodations.

♥

You can get some STDs, like herpes and genital warts, without having sex. Skin-to-skin contact with an infected area alone is sometimes enough to transfer the viruses.

> # Some STDs, like gonorrhea, can infect your eyes.

Government agencies and nonprofit organizations sometimes try to educate young people about diseases through comic books. In 1991 a comic book funded by the Ford Foundation tried to get people to pay attention to STD prevention by chronicling crime fighters "Captain Condom" and "Lady Latex" as they fought villains like "Admiral AIDS" and "Sergeant Syphilis." In the comic, just before a young man is about to have sex with his girlfriend, he says, "Yeah, this body is freak ripe!" To which she replies, "Ooh! This honey is hot!" After Lady Latex warns the woman about her lover's disease, the young man says, "Damn! My thing was ready to roll and now she's rolling out! Guess I better take their advice and pay that clinic a visit."

♥

Before the mid-19th century, most condoms were made from animal intestines.

> Condoms typically contain a milk protein, so some companies are launching vegan condoms that are free of animal products.

Similar to how Fleming accidentally stumbled upon penicillin, the discovery of rubberized dome covers was also a shot in the dark. Charles Goodyear was searching for a way to prevent rubber from freezing and cracking, but everything he tried melted. According to legend, he accidentally left rubber and sulfur on a hot stove. To everyone's surprise this prevented rubber from melting, while keeping its elasticity. The vulcanization of rubber led to many new products such as Goodyear tires, but it also affected the way people had sex because it revolutionized how condoms could be made and distributed. Vulcanized rubber led the way for cheaper and more effective contraception. Goodyear himself advertised that his new invention could be used for "nipple shields" and "gonorrhea bags."

♥

Population Services International (PSI) took heat for a condom ad it ran in 2007 in Botswana, which had one of the highest

HIV rates in the world at the time. The ad featured a 14-year-old girl with the caption, "I am going out with an older man who adds flavor to my life and one thing I do is have protected sex using Lovers Plus condoms every time [sic]." Since having sex with a girl under age 16 is a criminal offense in Botswana, PSI eventually pulled the ad.

♥

Anti-condom stances have become synonymous with the Catholic Church, which is interesting considering that the first written description of modern condoms comes from a Catholic clergy member. Gabriele Falloppio, also referred to as Fallopius, wrote about condoms in the 16th century claiming to have tested a linen sheath wrapped around the penis to prevent syphilis. He claimed to have tested the condom on more than 1,000 men and allegedly none contracted the syph. Although he was a cleric, Fallopius recommended the linen sheaths as a way to prevent STD transmission. He also described a tube that connects the ovary to the uterus. That tube of course is the fallopian tube, named in his honor. It might seem crazy today, but a cleric was the first person we have on record describing condoms, recommending them even, and later had a piece of female anatomy named after him.

♥

Cities that don't play by the porn industry's rules risk losing its lucrative tax revenue. Due to concerns that HIV was being transmitted on porn sets, Los Angeles County stipulated in 2012 that porn actors wear condoms when filming. The county subsequently saw a 95 percent drop in porn permit requests over the next 4 years.

Meanwhile, the number of total film productions in Las Vegas, where condoms were not required, jumped 50 percent from 2012 to 2013. Several observers attributed this to the condom law nudging porn production companies to leave LA for Vegas.

Between August and November of 2018, Trojan condoms was the second most popular producer of sandwich videos on YouTube.

According to Guinness, the largest condom in recorded history stood 72 feet high and shrouded the Luxor Obelisk in Paris on World AIDS Day in December 1993. The largest condom collection belongs to Amatore Bolzoni of Italy, who, over the course of a quarter century, amassed 2,077 different condoms. His oldest condom is from the 19th century and is derived from a sheep's bowel.

CHAPTER 5
PORN

When browsing porn, straight men search for penises about as often as they search for vaginas.

♥

The microfiche that libraries rely on to archive materials has its roots in Stanhopes, which are 19th-century optical devices that let people see microscopic photos without having to use a microscope. Making images microscopic meant that they could be viewed discreetly, so it isn't terribly surprising that this lent itself to pornography and that Stanhopes were often used to view erotic photos. If it weren't for people wanting to hide nudie pics, our archiving abilities would be worse off.

♥

Some scholars say that the first definition of the term "pornography" came in 1857 when a medical dictionary defined the word as a "description of prostitutes or of prostitution, as a matter of public hygiene."

♥

One of the planks of President Richard Nixon's political platform was his "crusade against the obscene." How dismayed he must have been when the man who took him down by feeding *Washington Post* reporters information about the Watergate burglary was codenamed Deep Throat.

♥

In 1967, President Lyndon Johnson set up the "President's Commission on Obscenity and Pornography" to study the effects of porn on society. Although the commission concluded that porn was not a big social problem and that Americans should focus more on improving sex education than on legislating obscenity, two men were sentenced to jail on obscenity charges for publishing an "illustrated" version of the commission's report.

♥

President Ronald Reagan also set up a commission to study porn. This commission concluded that porn harmed society by causing rape, facilitating prostitution, and being linked to organized crime. Reagan's team recommended that states change obscenity verdicts from misdemeanors to felonies. One of its commissioners, Rev. Bruce Ritter, suggested the government condemn pornography as well as homosexuality—before it came to light that he used funds from a charity he founded to solicit sex with young male prostitutes.

♥

Reagan's porn group became known as the Meese Commission, named after then US Attorney General Edwin Meese. Their report condemning porn was actually quite pornographic itself, describing sex acts in vivid detail. Some religious bookstores who supported the report's conclusions refused to stock the report on their shelves because they found it to be too vulgar. Feminist activist Susie Bright quipped, "I masturbated to the Meese Commission Report, until I nearly passed out—it's the filthiest thing around! And they know it." Regarding the report, an ACLU lawyer said, "I fully defend my government's right to publish filth."

Reed Smoot, a Mormon US senator out of Utah who served as a legislator during the early 1900s, really hated porn. His fight against porn led to an amazing newspaper headline: "Smoot Smites Smut."

> Diane Black, a US congresswoman out of Tennessee, tried to blame porn as a "root cause" of school shootings.

A Danish porn site held a contest where it asked its viewers to send in pictures of their dicks. The person with the smallest dick was rewarded with a free iPhone.

Smutty video games have been around as long as video games have existed. The Atari 2600 had a game called Beat 'Em and Eat

'Em where the purpose of the game was to move naked women across a street to catch falling semen in their mouths that was coming from a guy masturbating on top of a roof.

Many academic studies examining porn's effect on arousal and aggression are flawed. Several studies involve gathering a group of college students into a room, issuing them a questionnaire about their sexual attitudes, showing them some porn, and then issuing them another questionnaire about their sexual attitudes. The researchers then examined the differences in responses between the two surveys to see how porn affects people's behavior. But few people watch porn this way. In the real world, porn use is often coupled with a masturbation-driven release. As the economist Steven Landsburg wrote, "The experience of viewing porn on the Internet, in the privacy of one's own room, typically culminates in a slightly messier but far more satisfying experience—an experience that could plausibly tamp down some of the same aggressions that the pornus interruptus of the laboratory tends to stir up."

Economists from Carnegie Mellon and MIT took a more creative approach to studying sexual decision making by showing male study participants erotic photographs and having the experimental group in their study masturbate while they answered survey questions. The researchers found that when participants were aroused, they became more likely to report that they would have sex without a condom, lie in order to get laid, and persist in having sex with someone after they said no.

♥

If government researchers are the inventors of the internet, then pornographers are the entrepreneurs who brought it to the masses. The internet gave people a way to privatize their unmentionable habits, which is why porn users were willing to put up with the annoyances of the early days of online browsing and shopping. Because of this dynamic, ecommerce, video streaming, affiliate marketing, and online credit card transactions were popularized by pornographers. Porn also contributed to a lot of the bad crap you encounter online, too, such as spam, copyright infringement, chargebacks, ad fraud, and piracy. Since it dominated the flow of images and videos in the internet's early days, porn also drove the demand for more bandwidth, which was needed for the internet to become mainstream. Because porn is usually discussed in highly ideological ways, it's difficult for people to objectively examine its influence on the many products and services that guide our everyday lives.

> The porn industry keeps innovating. Computer-controlled sex toys, virtual reality, and sex avatars are just a few of the emerging technologies that porn execs are tinkering with.

Congress inadvertently encouraged people to use credit cards when purchasing porn online because the Communications Decency Act, which was intended to regulate digital porn, endorsed using credit cards to verify people's age. According to *Forbes*, "Though the act was overturned by the Supreme Court, porn operators are still shielded from accusations of peddling obscene material to minors so long as they require a credit card."

The Communications Decency Act that helped turn people on to using credit cards to purchase porn online was part of the broader Telecommunications Act of 1996. In 2000, pornographers took a bite out of the Telecommunications Act when Playboy won a US Supreme Court case that resulted in the elimination of the requirement that cable providers have to scramble channels that broadcast "sexually-oriented programming."

Because free speech battles are often won in the gutter, porn is a ripe place for First Amendment activism. In 1946, *Esquire* magazine won a US Supreme Court case against the United States Postal Service after a postmaster revoked its second-class mailing privileges because the magazine contained salacious photos of women. The "right to privacy" that pops up throughout US law was bolstered in part by a 1969 SCOTUS case that ruled it was unconstitutional to prohibit people from privately owning obscene material and that Georgia police didn't have the right to arrest a man for merely possessing porn.

♥

The raiding of an Oregon adult bookstore in 1982 culminated in the Oregon Supreme Court striking down obscenity laws in its state. Larry Flynt and *Hustler* magazine won a 1988 SCOTUS case against Jerry Falwell that made it more difficult for public figures to win lawsuits against people who mock or criticize them. This case became the basis of the critically acclaimed movie *The People vs. Larry Flynt*.

♥

Collectively, porn's court victories have expanded what can be legally broadcast, sent through the mail, and privately owned. And they've given more protections to media companies and satirists who aim to expose powerful figures.

♥

Hustler magazine publisher Larry Flynt wants obscenity to remain illegal. This seems counterintuitive as Flynt has spent decades battling obscenity charges and his magazine has come under fire for featuring outlandish centerfolds such as an image of a women being processed in a meat grinder with a meat inspection stamp that said, "Prime Grade 'A' Pink." Though Flynt thinks obscenity laws insult human intelligence, he doesn't want them overturned because if that happened be believes his business would suffer. Flynt believes that porn would lose its vice status and people would no longer pay much attention to it. In less than a decade, the industry would shrink dramatically and, according to Flynt, "the whole bottom would drop out of the porn market."

> After Denmark overturned its obscenity laws in 1969 and became the first state in modern history to rid all legal sanctions against porn, a researcher polling Copenhagen residents wrote, "The most immediate reaction to a one-hour pornography stimulation was boredom."

♥

Porn use is so prevalent that it prevented a University of Montreal study from ever starting. The researchers wanted to examine men who never watched porn, but they had to stop the study because finding participants was impossible. "We started our research seeking men in their twenties who never consumed pornography," one of the researchers told reporters. "We couldn't find any."

♥

Many people get festive with their porn watching. According to Pornhub research, searches for leprechaun porn surge during St. Patrick's Day and Santa-themed porn is popular during Christmas.

♥

A US government geological survey network became infected with malware because a government employee was watching a ton of porn on his work computer.

♥

The US Justice Department website AmberAlert.com is normally used by law enforcement officials to gather information about missing children. Unfortunately, the website became compromised by porn bots in spring 2018. People who visited the Amber Alert site were being redirected to porn web pages.

♥

A tired joke about *Playboy* magazine is that people bought it for its articles, not its nude photos, since the magazine featured acclaimed writers like Truman Capote, Joyce Carol Oates, and

Ray Bradbury, who serialized his novel *Fahrenheit 451* in the pages of *Playboy*. For former FBI director J. Edgar Hoover, the joke actually rang true. After *Playboy* began making fun of Hoover, the FBI head became obsessed with the magazine and kept close tabs on its founder Hugh Hefner. One FBI report notes that Hoover and his agents "have been reviewing the 'editorial credo' written by Hefner."

> **Playboy hosted its first White House Correspondents' Dinner Party in 2018.**

Playboy founder Hugh Hefner never masturbated until he was 18, and didn't lose his virginity until 22. Hef didn't begin his swinging ways until his first wife cheated on him. The affair devastated him and Hefner has admitted to overcompensating in response.

♥

The most iconic porn magazine in the world got rid of its nudes. *Playboy* stopped publishing pictures of naked women in 2016 in an effort to appeal to a broader audience. That did not work as planned, so they brought the nudes back the following year. But now Playboy is considering shuttering the magazine altogether since it loses as much as $7 million a year, and the company wants to pivot from publishing to brand licensing.

CHAPTER 6
POLITICS AND LAW

As an infamous brothel owner and star of the HBO show *Cathouse*, Dennis Hof was not a typical state legislature candidate. Nonetheless, Hof won a Republican primary for a Nevada state legislature seat just before he died after a night of partying at age 72. Hof's dead body was first discovered by a friend, the porn star Ron Jeremy. Although Hof was deceased in the run-up to the general election, he still won the race.

Roman lawmakers didn't beat around the bush when expressing their opinions. In enforcing legal monogamy, the ancient Roman jurist Gaius said that if a man had multiple wives, the wives should be perceived as "harlots" whose children are "spurious bastards conceived through promiscuous intercourse."

Lawmakers in Egypt tried to ban fake hymens that were imported from China. When pierced, the membrane-like products, which are inserted into vaginas, ooze a substance that looks like blood. These products can be helpful to women in the region whose husbands insist that they "prove" their virginity.

♥

There is no evidence that children are more likely to be targeted by sexual predators on Halloween than they are on any other day of the year. Nonetheless, in 2018 the mayor of Grovetown, Georgia, ordered sex offenders who are on probation in that area to report to City Hall on Halloween so that they could be detained while kids were out trick-or-treating.

> Calimesa, California passed a city ordinance that prohibits convicted sex offenders from displaying Halloween decorations on their home.

In 17th-century France, divorce was not permitted, but a marriage could be annulled legally if the union went unconsummated. This dynamic led to the rise of "impotence trials" where couples were subjected to public questioning by lawyers and gropings by medical professionals who wanted to determine if the husband could get it up. Marriages were legally dissolved after prosecutors concluded that the man in question was impotent. In some instances, these supposedly impotent men went on to remarry and father children with their second wives.

Russian empress Catherine the Great did not die from having sex with a horse, which was a rumor circulated by her enemies that is still believed by some people to this day. A true sex fact about Catherine the Great is that she owned some pretty radical furniture, such as chairs decorated with small sculptures of women's vulvas.

The way countries define marriage can impact crime rates since polygamous societies generally have more crime than monogamous societies. In a study of 157 countries published by the Royal Society, researchers found that legalizing polygamy leads to a greater number of unmarried men, which in turn contributes to higher rates of rape and murder. They concluded this is largely because single men are more likely to commit crimes than attached men.

A similar effect is found in societies where the gender ratio is skewed and there are more men than women. As China's gender ratio became more unbalanced, its crime rates rose. One study published by the Institute of Labor Economics concluded that "the increasing maleness" of China's population may account for a third of its overall rise in crime.

♥

The United States passed its first eugenics law in 1907 after an Indiana physician sterilized more than 450 inmates, claiming that he cured them of uncontrollable masturbatory urges and other alleged neurological disorders. As other eugenics laws popped up in other states, the US Supreme Court upheld their legality with its ruling in the 1927 case *Buck v. Bell*. After WWII, Nazi war criminals cited these laws in their defense.

♥

Sometimes organizations change their names after they've become inherently intertwined with human atrocities. For instance, the Catholic Church's Congregation for the Doctrine of the Faith used to be called the Supreme Sacred Congregation of the Roman and Universal Inquisition until the Inquisition became bad branding. This concept applies to sexual and reproductive groups, too. The American Eugenics Society renamed itself the Society for the Study of Social Biology and the academic journal *Eugenics Quarterly* became *Social Biology*.

♥

A biological sexual phenomenon is named after a US president. "The Coolidge Effect," named after President Calvin Coolidge, is when mammals show more sexual interest whenever they come across a new partner. Coolidge became synonymous with the effect because of a story that is likely apocryphal. The story goes that the president and his wife were on a farm and they noticed a rooster intensely mating with a hen. Mrs. Coolidge asked the farmhand how often this happens and the farmhand said dozens of time each day. "Tell that to the president," Mrs. Coolidge said. Mr. Coolidge then asked the farmhand if it was the same hen every time and when the farmhand acknowledged that the rooster mated with a different bird each time it mated, the president replied, "Tell that to Mrs. Coolidge."

> Former US Secretary of State Henry Kissinger once remarked, "Power is the ultimate aphrodisiac."

One of the first major sex scandals in United States politics involved Alexander Hamilton, the first secretary of the treasury and namesake of the award-winning Broadway play. Hamilton was sleeping with a married woman and paid her husband to keep quiet about the arrangement. His affair was exposed by pamphleteer James Callender, who would later go on to expose the relationship that President Thomas Jefferson had with Sally Hemings, who was his slave and a half-sister to Jefferson's late wife.

♥

In the United States, a law still exists on the books that technically makes it illegal to transport someone across state lines for the purposes of having sex with them. The Mann Act was originally launched during a moral panic in the early 1900s and was intended to reduce prostitution, but the law is worded so vaguely that it has been used by political opportunists and blackmailers to arrest people for merely having consensual sex with their significant others.

♥

During the 1920s, Nebraska adopted a law to castrate sex offenders. The law was not repealed for several decades.

♥

When US senator John McCain died from brain cancer, NBC interrupted a rerun of *America's Got Talent* to announce the solemn news. Immediately upon returning to its regularly scheduled programming, NBC broadcasted a clip of two large men in dolphin suits pretending to be making love. The odd juxtaposition left many wondering whether NBC did this on porpoise.

> **President Lyndon Johnson liked to call his penis "Jumbo."**

After reading affidavits related to the sexual harassment suit that Paula Jones filed against former President Bill Clinton, the British newspaper *The Independent* was not shy about painting a picture of Clinton's dong for its readers. The paper reported, "His erect penis is about 5 inches long, has the circumference of a quarter, and heads off at an angle, presumably rather like a finger bent at the joint."

♥

President Warren Harding had a mistress named Carrie Fulton Phillips whose vagina he nicknamed "Mrs. Pouterson."

♥

According to porn star Stormy Daniels, who claims to have had an affair with Donald Trump, the 45th president of the United States of America has a penis that looks like the mushroom-shaped character Toad from the Mario video game series.

♥

President Donald Trump—a man who has been on the cover of *Playboy*, appeared in a softcore porn film, cheated on each of his three wives, allegedly had an affair with a porn star he tried to pay off, and been accused of sexual harassment by at least 19 women—is lobbying for abstinence-only education and vowing to crack down on internet porn.

> **The only 2 US presidents to have been divorced are Donald Trump and Ronald Reagan.**

As he mounted an unsuccessful campaign to become governor of Kansas in 1932, John Brinkley made a fortune by stuffing goat testicles into human testicles. Brinkley, who advertised himself to customers as a qualified medical practitioner, claimed that goat glands could cure impotence and a series of other ailments. People desperate for cures during the Great Depression believed Brinkley and they paid him $500 (over $8,000 in 2018 dollars) to castrate goats and stuff the animal's testicles into a slit that Brinkley cut into the scrotum of his human patients. More than 100 of Brinkley's patients died due to infections brought on by his quack surgeries.

> Because the press used to protect presidents' personal lives in exchange for personal information, many Americans are unaware that Franklin Roosevelt had affairs. Because Roosevelt was paralyzed by polio, his friend allegedly asked FDR's doctor, "Is the president potent?" The doctor replied, "It's only his legs that are paralyzed."

Michigan state representative Lisa Brown got banned by her lawmaker colleagues from speaking on the floor after she said the word "vagina" during an abortion debate. To protest her banishment, Brown teamed up with the creator of the play *The Vagina Monologues*, Eve Ensler, and together they performed the play in front of the Michigan state capitol.

The Mitten State had one of the most bizarre political sex scandals in history. Michigan state legislators Todd Courser and Cindy Gamrat were having an affair while they both were in office. Once the news about their romance started circulating, Courser got the brilliant idea for a distraction. Courser told his staffers to start spreading a rumor that he was having sex with a male prostitute. His strategy was to "inoculate the herd" and spread really outrageous rumors so that people would begin doubting anything they hear about Courser's sex life. It did not work. Courser and Gamrat got booted from office and then slapped with felony charges for perjury and misconduct in office.

A 2011 report by Saudi Arabia's legislative assembly claimed that allowing women to drive would lead to "no more virgins" in the country. One of the conclusions found in the report is that making it legal for women to drive would "provoke a surge in prostitution, pornography, homosexuality, and divorce." At the time of the report, Saudi Arabia was the only country in the world that banned women from driving. In 2018, Saudi Arabia lifted its ban on women drivers.

> The first robot brothel in the US was set to open in Houston, but Houston city council members banned businesses in their jurisdiction from charging patrons to bang dolls that look like humans.

The US has never had an out gay person as its president, but some historians believe that James Buchanan may have been gay. Buchanan is the only American president to never marry and he lived with William Rufus King, the vice president under Franklin Pierce, who was the only vice president to remain a bachelor. When King moved to Paris, Buchanan wrote to him: "I am now 'solitary and alone,' having no companion in the house with me. I have gone a wooing to several gentlemen, but have not succeeded with any one of them. I feel that it is not good for man to be alone; and should not be astonished to find myself married to some old maid who can nurse me when I am sick, provide good dinners for me when I am well, and not expect from me any very ardent or roman-tic affection." A sexual relationship between the two men has not been definitively substantiated, but it is interesting that Buchanan could potentially be viewed as a gay icon.

♥

President John F. Kennedy's sex life reads like a soap opera involving affairs with famous actresses and interns. He reportedly once said, "I get a migraine headache if I don't get a strange piece of ass every day."

> **One book** alleges that Jackie Kennedy had an affair with movie star Marlon Brando, who may have made her an offer she couldn't refuse.

Candidates in the 2018 congressional race for the 5th district in Virginia ignited a fierce debate among politicos about the merits of "Bigfoot erotica."

♥

Ancient Rome disqualified people without children from holding some public offices.

In other societies, *not* having children helped advance people's political careers, as castrated men have held a lot of power in various societies throughout history. According to *Eunuchs and Castrati: A Cultural History*, eunuchs had an above-average life span, controlled administrations, held high-ranking civil positions, and formed cabinets that held real power within nations who had short-lived emperors. Because they were unable to have offspring, eunuchs were considered impartial and trustworthy, making them less likely to overthrow political dynasties than servants who were not castrated.

♥

When Sabna Nehru became the first eunuch politician to run for parliament in India, she told her critics: "You don't need genitals for politics. You need brains."

♥

Joni Ernst, a US senator from Iowa, got a big campaign boost after she aired a TV ad where she says, "I grew up castrating hogs on an Iowa farm, so when I get to Washington, I will know how to cut pork. . . . Washington is full of big spenders. Let's make them squeal."

♥

Lots of peculiar sex laws remain on the books even if they are no longer enforced. In Washington state you can lose your car for giving a sex worker a ride to work. Kisses should not last more than 5 minutes in Iowa. Arizona law states that a household cannot own more than 2 dildoes. In Michigan, it is technically illegal to cohabitate with a significant other who you are not married to. And in my great home state of Nebraska, you are technically not supposed to get married if you have gonorrhea.

> **Many states in the US lack laws banning necrophilia.**

CHAPTER 7
ECONOMICS

Many companies that seemingly have nothing to do with sex indirectly profit from it. Phone carriers like AT&T, satellite TV providers like DirecTV, and hotel chains like Marriott have earned millions by piping in smut to their customers. "It's the crazy aunt in the attic," an AT&T official told *The New York Times.* "Everyone knows she's there, but you can't say anything about it.'"

LGBT communities are known to be drivers of gentrification. They are more likely to want to live in urban cores, which tend to be more tolerant and culturally vibrant than rural areas. And since LGBT individuals are less likely to have children, they are less swayed by the state of local school districts when choosing where to live, a huge factor in cities where many families relocate to the suburbs because of failing public-school systems. Research has shown that LGBT residents have driven redevelopment in areas of many cities including Chicago, San Francisco, and Washington, D.C.

Some areas of Germany have a lot of old people with not enough working-age people to support them. To offset the worker shortage, the state once launched a program to convert prostitutes into eldercare nurses. A spokesperson for the program said "it was an obvious move" because the prostitutes have "good people skills, aren't easily disgusted, and have zero fear of physical contact. These characteristics can set former prostitutes apart from trainee nurses."

♥

A congressional war on phone sex sent some jobs overseas. In 1987, Congress introduced the "Telephone Decency Act," which made "obscene" and "indecent" phone calls illegal. "Dial-a-porn" company Sable Communications responded by suing the FCC for violating the First Amendment. Their case reached the Supreme Court, where the majority opinion stated, "Sexual expression which is indecent but not obscene is protected by the First Amendment." Although "indecent" phone calls were now made legal, the Court still upheld the ban on "obscene" phone communication. Rather than risk crossing the precarious legal zone between "indecent" and "obscene," phone sex providers looked to other countries for business. According to legal analyst Frederick Lane, in 1993 the island of São Tomé brought in $5.2 million worth of sex calls made by Americans being redirected to operators in São Tomé. The island's government made about half a million dollars from its share and used the money to build new telecommunications systems. By trying to stop Americans from having phone sex, Congress inadvertently sent phone sex jobs overseas to poorer nations. Nice.

"According to 2 separate groups of economists in the US and in Canada, raising taxes on alcohol leads people to consume less booze, which leads them to have less risky sex. One study shows that a I percent increase in beer price is associated with reducing gonorrhea rates by 0.8 percent."

Similar to the music industry's woes, piracy cut into porn's profits during the 2000s. Porn companies adapted by designing new business models around licensing, educational courses, live camming, crowdsourcing, event hosting, commerce, and creating custom packages in which consumers pay premiums to direct their own movies with porn stars. This multipronged approach is something that many struggling media companies could learn from.

> In a discovery that is much more correlation than causation, a researcher at the University of Helsinki found that between 1960 and 1985, countries whose men had smaller penises, on average, saw their GDP grow at a greater rate than countries whose men had long penises.

Before Social Security was in place in the United States, people expected their children to help take care of them in old age. But by rewarding residents the same amount of retirement payment regardless of whether or not they have any children, the incentive for having children has diminished. Economists estimate that Social Security can lower fertility rates by about 0.5 children per woman per lifetime.

Under Vladimir Putin, Russia created a few holidays aimed at getting people to have more babies. According to Jonathan Last, a journalist who studies demography, one holiday was "Family Contact Day," when workers were encouraged to leave the office to go home and bang. Another holiday was "Give Birth to a Patriot Day," and women who birthed children nine months after the holiday were eligible to win prizes like TVs and SUVs. South Korea, a country with low fertility rates, did something similar when its Ministry of Health began turning the office lights out early one Wednesday per month in an effort to get people to leave work and make love.

In 2012, Singapore hosted its "National Night" event, which encouraged young folks to "let their patriotism explode" since the country's policymakers wanted Singapore to reach a "population spurt it so desperately needs." The event was sponsored by Mentos, the fresh maker.

Denmark's birth rate is quite low, which spells trouble for its welfare system and economy. Danish travel agencies have taken it upon themselves to promote childbearing by promoting ads that urge parents to pay for vacations for their adult children. Presumably, people will have more sex on vacation, which will increase the chances of pregnancy, which will in turn save Denmark from its fertility issues.

♥

Because sex sells, it was only a matter of time before someone linked cryptocurrencies to sex acts. It should not be too surprising that there now exists a digital currency pegged to the "demand for synthetic rhino horn aphrodisiac pills."

> Executives from the clothing and apparel firm Under Armour let their employees know that, beginning in 2018, they were no longer allowed to pay for strip club visits with their company credit cards.

In the US, organizations that provide abortions also typically advocate for making contraception cheaply and easily accessible. Post-WWII Japan did not take this approach. Japan legalized abortion in 1948 before many other industrialized countries. It took another 50 years before the country legalized birth control pills in 1999. Some of the biggest opponents to legalizing oral contraception in Japan were Japanese abortion doctors, who worried that widespread use of the pill would reduce the number of abortions they perform, which would cut into their paychecks.

> Japan's population has aged quite dramatically and demographers predicted that by 2040, there will be more people over 100 years old in Japan than there will be newborn babies.

About 8.5 percent of the world's population is over 65 years old, according to The World Bank. In Japan, 27 percent of the population is older than 65, which is the highest rate in the world. The country's biggest diaper maker said that in 2011, it began selling more adult diapers than baby diapers. One Japanese family planning official warned that unless people in Japan start having more babies, the country "might eventually perish into extinction."

❤

China's 1-child policy led to a lot of invasive activity. To prove they were not pregnant, during the 1980s some female factory workers were forced to show that their menstrual products were stained.

♥

Where men significantly outnumber women, prostitution tends to proliferate. The evidence of this can be seen from contemporary China in the wake of the 1-child policy to 19th-century France, where industrialization brought on a wave of sex workers.

♥

China has a drastic shortage of women due to its 1-child policy. Hong Kong, on the other hand, has too few men, with fewer than 900 men for every 1,000 women. It is expected that by 2036 this gap will increase to 763 men for every 1,000 women. It would seem that the men in Hong Kong are in a dating market that statistically favors them, but cultural norms dictate that men are expected to marry women with lower earning power than them, which is a tough cookie for Hong Kong men to swallow since many of Hong Kong's women are educated, employed, and independent. Because of this dynamic, many men in Hong Kong bring in less-educated women from mainland China to marry. A demographer put it in straightforward, albeit depressing, terms: "Men at the bottom of society get left out of the marriage market, and that same pattern is coming to emerge for women at the top of society."

♥

Having too many men in a society can lead to economic problems. In China, the 1-child policy led to increased savings rates, according to a study by a Columbia University economist. This is because families with boys save more of their income to make their sons competitive in a dating market that statistically disadvantages them. "We found that not only did households with sons save more than households with daughters on average, but that households with sons tend to raise their savings rate if they also happen to live in a region with a more skewed gender ratio," said the study's author. The study estimated that half of the increase in household savings in China is attributable to parents saving money for mates for their sons. This means the 1-child policy holds economic significance because the high Chinese savings rate affects international trade imbalances.

CHAPTER 8
MILITARY

Eat your heart out, James Bond. Around WWI, a British intelligence officer used semen as invisible ink to write secret letters.

Penile plethysmography (PPG) tests track blood flow to the penis and are used as proxy measurements for sexual arousal. Police departments use them to punish sex offenders by gauging whether suspects are turned on by deviant material. This technology was developed by psychologist Kurt Freund in the 1950s for the Czech military, which wanted to be able to accurately identify homosexual men so that it could purge them. Czech officials recruited Freund because they were irritated that straight men were pretending to be gay so they would get kicked out of the service.

With their husbands off fighting in the Civil War, over 1,000 women in Nashville turned to prostitution to financially support themselves and their families. A military official responded to the growth in the number of sex workers by rounding them up and shipping them off to Louisville and Cincinnati, but when those cities ordered the ships full of hookers to head back where they came from, Union officials in Nashville decided they might as well try to make prostitution safe since it would inevitably occur. The result was the creation of America's first system of legalized prostitution.

♥

After assassinating Abraham Lincoln, John Wilkes Booth was killed by a religious Union Army soldier named Boston Corbett. Corbett said he killed Booth, despite receiving orders to take the assassin alive, because "God almighty directed me to." This was not the only time Corbett made a rash decision that he believed to be directed by God. Corbett was so devout that after getting turned on by the sight of a group of prostitutes, he went home and cut out his own testicles with a pair of scissors because he wanted to avoid sexual temptation and remain pure.

> Some folks have suggested that the term "hooker" is derived from the name of Civil War–era army officer Joseph Hooker because his squad really enjoyed the company of ladies of the night.

General John J. Pershing, commander of the American Expeditionary Forces in WWI, vocally supported the idea of an army free of venereal disease. He said that soldiers with VD were an "encumbrance to the army." Even though military generals at the time were outwardly critical of promiscuity, Pershing wasn't a great role model: he contracted gonorrhea twice as a serviceman.

> During the early 1900s, the War Department demanded that soldiers be sexually abstinent. In an effort to fight venereal disease, it issued pamphlets like one titled "Live Straight if You Would Shoot Straight" that stated "all loose women are dirty."

Venereal disease was so prevalent in the US military during the early 20th century that historians estimate the only thing causing soldiers to miss more days of combat was the influenza epidemic of 1918. An executive officer of a medical advisory board stated at the time: "If you were to attempt to get an army without having men who had gonorrhea, you would not have an army."

♥

After seizing Veracruz in the Pancho Villa Expedition, Red Cross nurses rounded up the area's prostitutes and inspected them for venereal disease. The US Army planned to regulate prostitution in the area and they needed to know which prostitutes were clean. As a surgeon at the time put it, "only those found uninfected were retained for duty." The specifications of prostitution during this campaign were so intense that some brothels were even segregated by race. One officer argued, "If prostitution were not provided, these men would disobey orders, go to Mexican villages, and get mixed up with the women and thereby possibly bring on war."

♥

The Hague Centre for Strategic Studies published an index of how inclusive militaries around the world are of LGBT people. New Zealand, which let its soldiers participate in a gay pride parade, ranked first out of the index's 103 countries. The United States ranked 40th just behind Romania. The ongoing battle of American politicians trying to ban transgender troops from serving in the military no doubt hampered the ranking of the United States.

> The US has been discharging soldiers for their sexuality ever since it declared independence. Lieutenant Gotthold Frederick Enslin, who was expelled from service in 1778, is believed to be the first person officially discharged for homosexuality.

Around the time of WWI, leading medical professionals like psychiatrist Albert Abrams believed that gay soldiers shouldn't be allowed to serve. To detect homosexuality in suspected gay troops, Abrams invented a device that was intended to record how much radiation came from people's junk. The theory was that gay men's balls would have less radiation than those of straight men.

♥

In 1919, secretary of the navy and future president FDR approved a "most searching and rigid investigation" into the gay subculture at the Newport naval base. The result of that investigation was lots of entrapment as enlisted men volunteered to go undercover at gay hangouts to catch gay sailors having sex. Some of the volunteer entrappers had sex with their fellow sailors only to later use that as "evidence" against the people they boned.

> As gay men were drummed out of the service around WWII, one method used to screen out gay service members involved pee. The idea was that gay troops undergoing urinary hormone tests would have more estrogen than their straight counterparts, but the tests became "too uncertain and too expensive to try on every inductee," according to *Newsweek* in 1947.

A WWI vet created the first LGBT rights organization in the United States. Many historians consider the Society for Human Rights, founded in 1924 by army vet Henry Gerber, to be the first LGBT rights organization in America. Veterans helped form several other early LGBT advocacy groups including the Veterans Benevolent Association.

♥

A pre-WWII policy led to an inordinate amount of lesbian service members. For a long time, married women were not allowed to enlist in the military and those who got pregnant were discharged. According to journalist Randy Shilts, these policies ensured that an inordinate number of women service members were lesbians. "The assumption became something of a self-fulfilling prophecy," Shilts wrote. "Young lesbians sometimes joined up specifically because they expected to find other lesbians in the military."

♥

At the time of WWII, a discharge for being gay outed people in an era when gay tolerance was incredibly low in the US. Instead of going home to hostile family and friends, many people discharged for being gay stayed in the port cities where they were removed from the army. This led to the growth of gayborhoods in several coastal cities like San Francisco and New York City. It is possible that without the military purging gay people, areas like the San Francisco Castro would not have become "gay Meccas."

> Some researchers have speculated that Rome legalized monogamy as a military tactic. Monogamy made it easier for lower-ranking soldiers to marry as it meant that elite males could not hoard a bunch of wives. Consistent sex would help satisfy the poor men and make them less likely to defect to other nations or start revolutions to overthrow the rich.

Although Greeks and Romans were the early adopters of the monogamy laws that are now prevalent across Western society, they made exceptions to the rules. When the Peloponnesian War left many men in the city dead, Athenian officials allowed for polygamy in an effort to rebuild its population.

♥

There is a fierce debate among some academic historians regarding whether or not Adolf Hitler had a micropenis.

> Mongolian conqueror Genghis
> Khan may have more than
> 16 million descendants.

French emperor Napoleon Bonaparte had a modest penis. At
1.5 inches in length, a *Time* magazine writer said that Bonaparte's
dick looked like a "maltreated strip of buckskin shoelace or a shriv-
eled eel" when it was displayed at the Museum of French Art in
Manhattan in 1927. An American man bought the package in an
auction in Paris in 1977 for $3,000.

CHAPTER 9
RELIGION

Ball-less male singers used to be in high demand. Handel, Mozart, and Monteverdi all wrote music intended for castrati. Even the Catholic Church preferred its singers to be without testicles. Under Pope Clement VII, the Sistine Chapel used castrati to serve the glory of God. It's estimated churches of Rome had about 100 castrati by the late 1600s and within 100 years the number doubled. The monastery of Monte Cassino had a center for castrating men. Castrati were designated as sopranos by the Vatican and also worked as theater actors. Some castrati earned international acclaim and helped popularize opera houses around Italy, sometimes making up as many as 7 of 10 voices in the opera.

Members of the Russian Christian sect Skoptzy cut off their genitals and breasts in their quest to sanctify themselves for the afterlife.

In a few predominantly Muslim countries, temporary marriages are condoned, and some people use these brief unions as religious cover for sexual pleasures that otherwise would be sinful.

Epidemiologist Elizabeth Pisani said that because of these temporary marriages, she has met prostitutes who have been married hundreds of times. "Good Muslim clients perform the wedding ceremony for themselves before starting in on the girl," Pisani writes. "An hour later, they divorce her. Since they were married while they were having sex, they have not sinned."

> To determine whether or not a piece of media should be declared legally obscene, English law relies on a test that was created during an 1868 case involving a Protestant activist who sold anti-Catholic pamphlets that described priests becoming sexually aroused during confessions.

There is a wide range in how countries legally treat gay and transgendered people. Iran takes an approach that many Westerners are likely to find peculiar, if not upsetting. In Iran, homosexuality is punishable by death. But the country allows for sex reassignment surgery because some Iranian clerics believe that people can become trapped in bodies of the wrong sex. There are gay people in Iran who aren't suffering from gender dysphoria who will seek out gender reassignment surgeries so that they can avoid being executed for being gay. In some cases, the government provides loans for the procedures, and there have been instances of government officials coercing people into having these surgeries.

> There is a pagan temple in Montreal devoted to penises that requires its members to play with dicks for 4 hours a week.

Greek gods have lent their name to several sex-related terms. Aphrodite, the goddess of love and beauty, is the namesake for aphrodisiac. Hermaphrodite's etymology is derived from combining the names Aphrodite and Hermes, the male messenger of the gods. Long-lasting erections, known as priapisms, get their name from the god of fertility, Priapus, who has an incredibly long schlong in paintings.

> Gardeners in ancient Rome used replicas of the fertility god Priapus as scarecrows hoping that the god's giant phallus would scare off birds.

When a pig in colonial Connecticut gave birth to a deformed piglet, it led Puritan colonists to execute a man named George Spencer because they believed Spencer created the deformity by having sex with the pig and fathering its offspring. The execution was justified on biblical grounds since Leviticus 20:15 stated that a person who has sex with an animal shall be put to death.

In Japan, an ancient Shinto fertility ritual has become an annual festival that celebrates giant dongs.

Holy men in Varanasi, India, cut holes into their penises and lodge sticks into them so that they can stretch their penises as an act of worship.

♥

In the Middle Ages, multiple influential Christian theologians stated that prostitution was a necessary evil. They relied on an analogy that equated streetwalkers with sewers, implying that they provided an outlet for filth, which helped society stay purer.

♥

According to a few Old Testament verses, a man having sex with his wife while she menstruates is a sin on par with committing adultery.

♥

During Christianity's early years, several theologians suggested that anal sex should require a stricter penance than homicide.

> When the Catholic Church sought to ban clerical marriage, some priests fought hard to retain their right to have a wife. In 1077 France, one proponent of clerical celibacy got burned alive by outraged clergy.

Catholic priests are supposed to be sexually abstinent, but some break their vows. According to The *Kansas City Star*, this explains why the AIDS death rate for American priests was about double the rate among adult males in the US after HIV awareness became widespread in the 1980s.

♥

It is possible that economics can influence people to make sexual sacrifices by enrolling in a seminary and foregoing carnal relations. One study found that a 1 percent increase in unemployment corresponded with a 3.5 percent increase in seminary enrollment. In hard economic times, jobs are hard to come by and the social services that churches provide are in high demand. "Historically, times of challenge or crisis usually bring out the best in people," said a US Conference of Catholic Bishops official. "We saw a huge boon in candidates to the priesthood after the Great Depression and WWII."

♥

Back in 1947, Rev. Gerald Fitzgerald founded the Congregation of the Servants of the Paraclete to deal with priests' behavioral problems, which included pedophilia. Bishops sent the Paracletes so many sexually abusive priests that Fitzgerald searched for a private island where the Catholic Church could harbor and isolate clergy sex offenders from society. Although the island never came to be, Fitzgerald was so serious about secluding clerical pedophiles that he eventually made a $5,000 down payment on a $50,000 Caribbean island that he wanted his archdiocese to purchase.

♥

"I know it when I see it," is probably the most-used phrase to define pornography, and it comes from Supreme Court Justice Potter Stewart's categorization of obscene material. In 2005, a US Conference of Catholic Bishops official made a nod to that phrase when a reporter asked him how seminary directors would enforce the Vatican's rule to ban men with "deep-seated homosexual tendencies" from the priesthood. "It's more like one of those things where it's hard to define," the official said. "But 'I know it when I see it.'"

♥

John Rock, coinventor of the pill, was a devout Catholic who opened the first clinic in Boston that taught the Church-approved "rhythm method." Given the Church had already approved the "rhythm method," Rock built off its logic and designed the pill around a 28-day cycle to mimic a woman's menstrual cycle in hopes of earning Church approval by aiming to make the contraceptive appear as "natural" as possible. But this is not medically necessary; it could have been any number of days.

> Monks at a Buddhist monastery in Bhutan use wooden phalluses to bless visitors who are seeking children.

During the Middle Ages, at least 12 different churches claimed they possessed Jesus's foreskin.

♥

When the Old Testament was written thousands of years ago, STDs were less treatable and caused infertility, birth defects in infants, and even death. It is possible that the Jewish men who wrote the earliest biblical books were influenced by their environment where STDS were deadly and misunderstood, which could lead one to suspect that God should punish sexual transgressors harshly. One theorist points out ancient cults that practiced sexual rituals as part of their religious service have died out while religions with lots of sexual restrictions survived. However, a religion can't have too many sexual restrictions if it is to survive. The Shakers are practically extinct because they believed that people should never have sex, which led to married Shakers never getting it on or having children to pass their culture on to.

> A Hindu astrology guide forecasts that men with big penises will be poor and have no sons.

Seeking out reproductive assistance can be tricky for women in the Middle East if their religion outlaws technologies that would help them have their own children. When that challenge arises, sometimes the unthinkable happens and people of different faiths come together to make a baby. The Sunni and Shia denominations of Islam have different approaches to reproductive technology. Sunnis using artificial insemination must be married before they do so and they are only allowed to use their own eggs and sperm in the process, but in Shia-majority countries like Lebanon and Iran, jurists have interpreted the Qur'an to favor the permissibility of using other people's eggs and sperm for reproduction. Because infertility is high and adoption is frowned upon in many Middle Eastern societies, some infertile Sunni couples venture into Shia territory to expand the reproductive techniques they can use to increase their probability of producing a child. In vitro fertilization attempts tend to fail more than 70 percent of the time, and the treatments are expensive, meaning that only the wealthy can afford them in many countries. While reproductive technology isn't always a savior, the women jumping borders to receive reproductive assistance demonstrate how cultural diversity can be personally beneficial.

CHAPTER 10
CULTURE

A study in the scientific journal *Current Biology* found that ancient eunuchs in Korea lived 14 to 19 years longer than other men. Researchers suspected the main culprit was that male sex hormones could reduce a man's life span by making him predisposed to heart attacks. The researchers cite this as evidence why females in many species, including humans, live longer than males. However, the research is mixed as other studies found no difference between eunuch life spans and other males. Nonetheless, cutting off your junk to lengthen your life is an interesting perspective to consider.

♥

Huffpost and YouGov polled 1,000 adults in the US and found that 9 percent of them would have sex with a robot. Apparently, the other 91 percent of respondents have not seen the movie *Ex Machina*.

♥

In Western countries, people go to tanning salons to make themselves look sexier, but this practice is baffling in other cultures. Across Asian countries like China and Korea, women use umbrellas on sunny days, take ski masks and "sun protection gloves" to the beach, and apply skin-lightening products to their bodies to ensure that their skin will not become too dark.

The sweat of gladiators was considered an aphrodisiac in ancient Rome.

Foods like oysters and bananas have been considered aphrodisiacs because they look like people's genitalia.

Ithyphallophobia is a long word that means fear of penises.

The Museum of Russian Erotica claims it has Grigori Rasputin's 13-inch dick, which it naturally houses in a jar for people to gawk at.

In 1994, a Tel Aviv ad agency gave a low blow to the egos of the city's bad drivers by releasing ads with the slogan: "Research proves aggressive drivers have small penises."

In general, the number of children that women from any given country bear on average tends to decline as the amount of education women receive increases. When more women in the US entered colleges during the early 1900s, so-called experts viewed this trend to be catastrophic. According to the famous psychologist G. Stanley Hall, higher education would make women "functionally castrated." A gynecologist at the time said that as more women went to college the number of "sexual incompetents" in the country would increase.

♥

A cliché often passed around is that the divorce rate in the US is "50 percent and climbing." This is utter nonsense. Divorce rates have actually declined considerably since the 1970s and 1980s when no-fault divorces initially become commonplace. In marriages that started in the 1990s, about 70 percent reached their 15th anniversary. In marriages that began in the 1970s and 80s, just 65 percent reached their 15th anniversary. The "50 percent and climbing" factoid comes from faulty statistics pushed by family-focused special-interest groups. It is not empirically valid.

In Japan, some married couples end their relationship with a divorce ceremony where they break their wedding rings with hammers.

People have taken all kinds of approaches to altering boobs. They've been compressed in seventh-century Spain, distended in Paraguay, and blown up to giant proportions in the United States.

♥

Male enhancement products litter the back pages of smutty magazines and late-night infomercials. Some dudes even go through painful surgeries to make their cocks bigger. The obsession with big dicks is not a universal human condition, however. For instance, the ancient Greeks found small penises to be the most beautiful kind of male appendage.

> There is a restaurant in China that specializes in genitals. The tiger penis entrée there costs more than $5,000.

People have gotten creative with how they utilize the sex organs of castrated men. One explorer wrote of dead soldiers having their genitals filled with straw and tacked onto spears. Castrati in China hoped their junk would come back in the afterlife. Since Confucianism taught that the body would be preserved after death, they kept severed penises in ornamental pouches, which would accompany them to their graves. A nomadic group of people in

Sudan wore the lopped-off penises of their enemies as necklaces. In southwestern Ethiopia, severed sex organs were sun-dried and worn as bracelets.

♥

Most researchers believe the amount of LGBT people is around 5 percent of the total population or less. Gallup estimates that 4.5 percent of people in the US are LGBT. Meanwhile, Gallup polls also show that more than a third of Americans believe that at least 25 percent of the population is gay.

♥

There is a tradition in parts of Greece and the Balkans where men dance with a handkerchief under their armpit so that they can present the scent to women they want to dance with.

♥

Modesty is a relative concept. Anthropologists report that indigenous women in the Amazon who only wear a thin cord around their waists show just as much anxiety removing their belts in public as US women do when they take off a blouse.

> Americans got married at younger ages in the 1950s than they did during the late 1800s.

Avocados get their name from the Aztec word "āhuacatl," which was used to describe both fruit and testicles.

♥

On the Indonesian island Lombok, prenuptial kidnappings are a thing. Prearranged marriages used to be the norm on the island. Over time, a tradition developed where a woman wouldn't have to marry the man her parents set her up with if she got kidnapped before the wedding. For couples who met outside of a parental arrangement, getting married involved the groom kidnapping the bride from her parents' house.

♥

The world's only known eunuch museum sits in a suburb outside of Beijing. Some of the most famous people in Chinese history, including the inventor of paper, Cai Lun, were eunuchs.

> ## US teens are having less sex than their parents' generation had.

Monogamy has been around for millennia, but it is just within the past few hundred years that most of the world's population has lived in cultures that legally enforce monogamy. This shift occurred when Japan, Thailand, Nepal, China, and India began prohibiting polygamy.

Most people live in monogamous societies, but few cultures practice monogamy as their default mating system. About 15 percent of the 1,200 cultures the Ethnographic Atlas Codebook analyzed were monogamous.

♥

There is a stereotype that married people have stale sex lives, but these tired jokes overlook the fact that married folk have regular access to a sexual partner that many singles envy. For what it's worth, researchers find that married people have more sex than single people. And they report that their sex is more satisfying, too.

♥

Just 0.2 percent of marriages in the United States today are between first or second cousins, but cousin marriage was much more popular in the past when humans lived in smaller societies and did not travel far from where they were born. A Rutgers anthropologist claims that about 80 percent of all marriages in human history have been between first and second cousins.

♥

"Double cousins" is where two siblings from one family marry two siblings of another family. North Carolina legally prohibits these types of marriages even though people share no biological relation to their in-laws' siblings. But the Tar Heel State does allow people to marry their first cousins whom they are actually related to.

♥

The cynic Greek philosopher Diogenes hated social conventions. He showed his contempt for rules by jerking off in public marketplaces. While this is an interesting way to protest authority, it is unlikely to get you out of your parking ticket.

♥

Yes, there is a penis shrine in Bangkok.

♥

In medieval Europe, men liked to wear long, pointy shoes as there was a belief that foot size correlated with penis size. Some guys even stuffed their shoes with sawdust so that their footwear would stand erect.

♥

A lot of guys are under the impression that women love big penises, but not all women prefer a big dong. One woman from Zimbabwe sued her ex-boyfriend because he allegedly stretched out her vagina with his long penis. The woman wanted her ex to pay nearly $10,000 for a reconstructive surgery to make her vagina tight again. It remains unclear just how large the man's penis is.

> Filipino seamen slit their penises and insert small plastic or stone balls into them to enhance the size.

A 22-year old man in Scotland had his genitals "ripped off and eaten" by a bulldog named Biggie Smalls after the man applied peanut butter to his scrotum.

♥

An environmentalist from Peru took tree hugging a little too literally by marrying a tree in 2014.

♥

Boys in an aboriginal group in Australia undergo a manhood initiation ceremony where they swallow their own foreskin.

♥

There is a form of martial arts that involves using genitals to lift heavy weights.

> A 69-year-old Dutch man launched a lawsuit to reduce his legal age by 20 years because he felt that age was fluid like gender and he would have an easier time getting laid on dating apps if he identified as a 49-year-old.

After the digital news and entertainment site Gawker published a sex tape of pro-wrestling icon Hulk Hogan screwing his friend's ex-wife, Hogan sued the website out of existence. Gawker's lawyers argued that the sex life of Hogan—whose real name is Terry Bollea—was fair game for them to report on because Hogan was a public figure and he talked about his sexual prowess when promoting himself. Gawker lawyers referenced a 2006 radio clip where Hogan bragged about having a 10-inch wang. This led to a bizarre sequence in the courtroom where Hogan claimed he was referring to the penis size of the character "Hulk Hogan" and that in real life, his penis was not that big. "It's not mine," Hogan said, "because mine is not the size we're discussing." "Really?" one of Gawker's lawyers asked him in response. "No, seriously," Hogan said. "I do not have a 10-inch penis . . . Terry Bollea's penis is not 10 inches, like you're trying to say."

> Part of the reason why circumcision is popular in countries like the United States is because it was believed that it would reduce masturbation.

♥

Frankenstein author Mary Shelley allegedly lost her virginity on top of her mother's grave. She also kept the heart of her dead husband and carried it around with her.

SOURCES

INTRODUCTION

Joseph Henrich, Robert Boyd, and Peter Richerson, "The Puzzle of Monogamous Marriage," *Philosophical Transactions of the Royal Society B*: Biological Sciences, 367, no. 1589 (2012): 657–669, doi:10.1098/rstb.2011.0290.

Bill Powell, "Gender Imbalance: How China's One-Child Law Backfired on Men," *Newsweek*, May 28, 2015.

John Money, *The Destroying Angel: Sex, Fitness & Food in the Legacy of Degeneracy Theory, Graham Crackers, Kellogg's Corn Flakes & American's Health History* (New York: Prometheus, 1985).

Leonard Derogatis and Katherine King. "The Coital Coronary: A Reassessment of the Concept." *Archives of Sexual Behavior* 10, no. 4 (1981): 325–335, doi:10.1007/BF01565536.

Maggie Koerth-Baker, "Space Sex Is Serious Business," *FiveThirty-Eight*, March 14, 2017.

"Alabama Sex Toy Drive-Thru Business on the Rise," *Associated Press*, December 30, 2010.

John Troyer, "Abuse of a Corpse: A Brief History and Re-Theorization of Necrophilia Laws in the USA." *Mortality* 13, no. 2 (2008): 132–152, doi:10.1080/13576270801954518.

Katy Duke, "Project Retrains Prostitutes as Care Workers for Elderly People," *British Medical Journal* 332, no. 7542 (2006): 685, doi:10.1136/bmj.332.7543.685-a.

Piotr Scholz, *Eunuchs and Castrati: A Cultural History*, trans. Shelley Frisch and John Broadwin (Princeton NJ: Markus Wiener Publishers, 2001).

Ella Davies, "'Singing Penis' Sets Noise Record for Water Insect," *BBC Nature,* June 30, 2011.

Becky Little, "Shark Surprises Aquarium with Rare 'Virgin Birth,'" *National Geographic,* January 18, 2017.

Richard Rhodes, "Father of the Sexual Revolution," *New York Times,* November 2, 1997.

ANIMALS

Joseph Stromberg, "This Sea Slug Discards Its Penis after Sex and Grows Another," *Smithsonian,* February 13, 2013.

Ellen Airhart, "When Growing Their Penis for the Season, Ducks Bend to Social Pressure," *Popular Science*, September 20, 2017.

Bjon Carey, "The Painful Realities of Hyena Sex," *Live Science,* April 26, 2006.

Tia Ghose, "Schwing! Alligator Sports Always-Erect, Hidden Penis," *Live Science,* February 20, 2013.

Lucy Cooke, "Penguin Prostitution Is a Thing," *The Atlantic,* June 2018.

Ella Davies, "'Singing Penis' Sets Noise Record for Water Insect," *BBC Nature,* June 30, 2011.

Sara Chodosh, "Fun Facts About Giraffe Sex to Keep You Occupied While You Wait for That Giraffe Baby," *Popular Science,* March 1, 2017.

Matt Simon, "Absurd Creature of the Week: This Marsupial Has Marathon Sex until It Goes Blind and Drops Dead," *Wired,* May 2, 2014.

Ella Davies, "Labord's Chameleons of Madagascar Live Fast, Die Young," *BBC Earth News,* February 21, 2011.

Dana Dovey, "Insect Sex: Watch Headless Praying Mantis Continue to Mate after Being Decapitated by Female," *Newsweek,* November 17, 2017.

Matt Simon, "Absurd Creature of the Week: This Slug Has Such a Big Penis It Has to Mate Upside Down," *Wired,* September 25, 2015.

Sarah Tung, "Top 10 Weird Insect Mating Rituals," *Time,* August 16, 2010.

Felicity Morse, "Valentine's Day: The Animals That Don't Do Romance," *BBC Newsbeat,* February 13, 2015.

James Vaughn Kohl and Robert Francoeur, *The Scent of Eros: Mysteries of Odor in Human Sexuality* (New York: Authors Choice Press, 1995), 36.

"Professor Wins Ig Nobel Prize For Beer, Sex Research," *ScienceDaily,* September 29, 2011.

Patricia Edmonds, "The Weird World of Lobster Sex," *National Geographic,* July 2017.

Nadia Drake, "Can't Burn This: DNA Shows Surprising Flame-Retardant Properties," *Wired,* March 11, 2013.

Ker Than, "Barnacles Can Change Penis Size and Shape," *National Geographic News,* February 13, 2008.

"There Is a Type of Duck That Sometimes Lassos Its Potential Mates with Its Penis," *Today I Found Out,* October 14, 2011.

Andy Coghlan, "Female Ducks Fight Back Against 'Raping' Males," *New Scientist,* May 1, 2007.

Ed Yong, "How Chickens Lost Their Penises (and Ducks Kept Theirs)," *National Geographic,* June 6, 2013.

Ella Davies, "Bloodless Erections for Big Birds, Say Researchers," *BBC Nature,* December 12, 2011.

Ryan Haupt, "Kangaroos' Triple Vaginas Make You Feel Like an Inefficient Unitasker," *Motherboard,* April 20, 2012.

Esther Inglis-Arkell, "Why Do Snakes Have a Hemipenis?," *io9,* June 15, 2015.

Ryan Smith, "How Noisy Males Control the Gnu's Cycle," *Smithsonian,* July 11, 2018.

Ellen Byron, "Big Cats Obsess over Calvin Klein's 'Obsession for Men,'" *Wall Street Journal,* June 8, 2010.

Natalie Zarrelli, "How to Seduce a Turkey: The Bizarre Poultry Sex Experiments of the 1960s," *Atlas Obscura,* November 24, 2015.

Ed Yong, "Crows Sometimes Have Sex with Their Dead," *The Atlantic,* July 18, 2018.

David Shultz, "Everything You Always Wanted to Know About Dolphin Sex—But Were Afraid to Ask," *Science Magazine,* April 23, 2017.

Yasmin Tayag, "Humans Might Be to Blame for Lonely, Horny Dolphin's Unwanted Advances," *Inverse,* August 29, 2018.

Robert Britt, "Monkeys Pay to See Female Monkey Bottoms," *Live Science,* January 28, 2005.

Monica Heisey, "The Infuriating Hubris of Men Who Want to Donate Their Dicks to a Penis Museum," *Broadly,* April 3, 2018.

Alan Burdick, "Elegy for the World's Oldest Spider," *New Yorker,* May 5, 2018.

Patricia Edmonds, "Armadillo Courtship Is the Joy of the Chase—and the Catch," *National Geographic,* July 2018.

Ron Kotulak and Jon Van, "Prairie Voles' Mating Rituals Are Nothing to Sniff At," *Chicago Tribune,* May 21, 1995.

Matt Soniak, "Are Rabbits as Prolific as Everybody Says?," *Mental Floss,* January 20, 2015.

Jamie Havrila et al., "Are You Paying Attention? Female Wolf Spiders Increase Dragline Silk Advertisements When Males Do Not Court," *Ethology* 121, no. 4 (2014): 345–352, doi:10.1111/eth.12340.

Ben Panko, "This Worm Hasn't Had Sex in 18 Million Years," *Smithsonian,* October 18, 2017.

Joseph Castro, "Pregnant Monkeys Miscarry to Avoid Infanticide," *Live Science,* February 23, 2012.

Kenneth Souza, Shaun Black, and Richard Wassersug, "Amphibian Development in the Virtual Absence of Gravity," *Proceedings of the National Academy of Sciences* 92, no. 6 (1995):1975–1978, doi:10.1073/pnas.92.6.1975.

"Pregnant Rats in Space Face Births on Earth," *Associated Press,* November 9, 1994.

Joshua Rapp Learn, "Why Snail Sex Is Like a Box of Chocolates," *Smithsonian,* July 20, 2017.

Cecile Borkhataria, "Small Birds Form 'Mobs' and Launch Dive-Bombing Attacks on Larger Predators to Impress Females," *Daily Mail,* February 22, 2017.

"My Pet—The Pet Record Maker," App Annie, accessed June 18, 2018.

"Puppy Planner—Heat Cycle," Apple Store Preview, accessed June 18, 2018.

Alan Yuhas, "Russia Confirms Death of Five Geckos on Space Sex Mission," *The Guardian*, September 1 2014.

Becky Little, "Shake Surprises Aquarium With Rare 'Virgin Birth,'" *National Geographic*, January 18, 2017.

Michelle Douglass, "Shark Sets New Sperm Storage," *BBC*, January 9, 2015.

Katie Langin, "Exclusive: 'I've Never Seen Anything Like It.' Video of Mating Deep-sea Anglerfish Stuns Biologists," *Science Magazine*, March 22, 2018.

Andres Lopez-Sepulcre, "Beyond Lifetime Reproductive Success: The Posthumous Reproductive Dynamics of Male Trinidadian Guppies," *Proceedings of the Royal Society B* 280, no. 1763 (2013), doi:10.1098/rspb.2013.1116.

"Male Bats Trade Brains for Better Odds at Sex," *Associated Press*, January 24, 2006.

Gavin Butler, "Fish Could Be Getting High and Horny Off Our Wastewater Drugs," *Vice*, October 17, 2018.

Kyle Buchanan, "You'll Never Guess How the Dinosaur Sounds in *Jurassic Park* Were Made," *Vulture*, June 9, 2015.

COMMERCIAL PRODUCTS

Mary Roach, *Bonk: The Curious Coupling of Science and Sex* (New York: W.W. Norton & Co., 2008), 142, 292.

Megan Gibson, "The Long, Strange History of Birth Control," *Time*, February 2, 2015.

Sophie Bushwick, "The Good-Old Days of Contraception: Lemon-Peel Diaphragms and Beaver-Testicle Tea," *Discover Magazine,* June 29, 2012.

Reegan Von Wildenradt, "Introducing Morning Glory, the Boner-Tracking App You Didn't Know You Needed," *Men's Health,* January 25, 2018.

"Fendi's £750 'Vulva' Scarf Makes Wearers Look Like They're Being Born," *The Guardian,* October 15, 2018.

Geoff Herbert, "'Oneida' Book Explores CNY Commune's Theory of Sexual Healing and Immortality," *The Post-Standard,* May 10, 2016.

Kasandra Brabaw, "These Vibrating Apps Turn Your Phone into a Sex Toy," *Refinery29,* November 6, 2018.

Lara Rutherford-Morrison, "Foods You Can Cook Using Semen, Because This is a Real Thing, Even If It Seems Like ~Came~ Out of Nowhere," *Bustle,* June 1, 2015.

Bartosz Staszewski, "Vagina Beer Made with 'Essence of Hot Underwear Models' Goes on Sale for First Time," *Daily Mirror,* August 2, 2018.

Gabe Bergado, "Bradley Charvet's Blowjob Cafe Will Also Serve Coffee," *Inverse,* November 22, 2016.

Gabrielle Okun, "Researcher Finds Bluetooth-Enabled Butt Plug Can Be Controlled from Anywhere," *Daily Caller,* October 18, 2017.

Kate Knibbs, "The Curious Case of Clorox's Bizarre Hookup App," *The Daily Dot,* April 1, 2014.

Kashann Kilson, "These Early Sex Toys Will Blow Your Mind, and That's Just for Starters," *Inverse,* December 3, 2015.

Rebekah Sager, "The Guy Who Played Barney the Dinosaur Now Runs a Tantric Sex Business," *Vice,* January 23, 2018.

Christopher Palmeri and Lucas Shaw, "Gwyneth Paltrow's Goop Pays $145,000 over Jade Vaginal-Egg Claims," *Bloomberg,* September 4, 2018.

"New Line of Blue Jeans Enhance Men's 'Assets,'" *Reuters,* November 9, 2001.

Chuck Shepherd, "News of the Weird," *Miami New Times,* April 9, 1998.

Sandra Pedicini, "Club Juana Closes after 43 Years," *Orlando Sentinel,* June 18, 2006.

James Jones, *Alfred C. Kinsey: A Life* (New York: W.W. Norton & Co., 1997), 572.

Lia Kvatum, "A Period Comes to an End: 100 Years of Menstruating Products," *Washington Post,* April 25, 2016.

"'Family Planning,' Vintage Disney Sex-Ed Film, Explains Almost Nothing," *Huffpost,* September 3, 2013.

"Walt Disney's Film for Kotex: The Story of Menstruation," The Museum of Menstruation, accessed July 10, 2018.

"A Long Overdue Disruption in Menstrual Products," *The Economist,* March 31, 2018.

Ema Sagner, "More States Move to End 'Tampon Tax' That's Seen as Discriminating Against Women," *NPR,* March 25, 2018.

Ann Friedman, "Astronaut Sally Ride and the Burden of Being the First," *The American Prospect,* June 19, 2014.

Jessica Kane, "Here's How Much a Woman's Period Will Cost Her over a Lifetime," *Huffpost,* May 18, 2015.

Elaine Glusac, "When PMS Punches, Go with the Crunches," *Chicago Tribune,* December 24, 1995.

J. R. Thorpe, "The History of the Tampon—Because They Haven't Always Been for Periods," *Bustle,* November 19, 2015.

Christopher Turner, *Adventures in the Orgasmatron: How the Sexual Revolution Came to America* (New York: Farrar, Straus and Giroux, 2011), 6.

Robin Baker, *Sperm Wars: Infidelity, Sexual Conflict, and Other Bedroom Battles* (New York: Thunder's Mouth Press, 1996), 102.

Robert Jutte, *Contraception: A History,* trans. Vicky Russell (Malden, MA: Polity Press, 2003), 34.

David Kennedy, *Birth Control in America: The Career of Margaret Sanger* (New Haven CT: Yale University Press, 1970), 115.

Christine Dehlendorf et al., "Disparities in Family Planning," *American Journal of Obstetrics & Gynecology* 202, no. 3 (2010): 214–220, doi:10.1016/j.ajog.2009.08.022.

Richard Reeves and Joanna Venator, "Sex, Contraception, or Abortion? Explaining Class Gaps in Unintended Childbearing," *Brookings*, February 26, 2015.

Julie Turner, "A Brief History of the Bikini," *Slate*, July 3, 2015.

Maureen O'Connor, "Top Notes of Poo," *New York Magazine*, July 24, 2018.

John Money, *The Destroying Angel: Sex, Fitness & Food in the Legacy of Degeneracy Theory, Graham Crackers, Kellogg's Corn Flakes & American's Health History* (New York: Prometheus, 1985), 84

Elizabeth Abbott, *A History of Celibacy: From Athena to Elizabeth I, Leonardo da Vinci, Florence Nightingale, Gandhi, & Cher* (New York: Scribner, 1999), 206.

Sylvester Graham, *A Lecture to Young Men on Chastity: Intended Also for the Serious Consideration of Parents and Guardians* (Boston: Light & Stearns, Crocker & Brewster, 1837), 78–80.

Rachel Maines, *The Technology of Orgasm: "Hysteria," the Vibrator, and Women's Sexual Satisfaction* (Baltimore: The Johns Hopkins University Press, 1999), 67–89.

Bethy Squires, "Doctors Created Vibrators after Growing Tired of Masturbating 'Hysterical' Women," *Broadly*, January 6, 2017.

Marlow Stern, "'Hysteria' and the Long, Strange History of the Vibrator," *The Daily Beast*, April 27, 2012.

Christopher Trout, "The 46-Year-Old Sex Toy Hitachi Won't Talk About," *Engadget*, October 27, 2014.

Drew Schwartz, "How One Sex Toy Fucked an Entire Airport," *Vice,* August 8, 2018.

Lauren Pastrana, "Viagra Saves Sex Lives and Children's Lives," CBS Miami, December 7, 2015.

Christopher Barnett and Roberto Machado, "Sildenafil in the Treatment of Pulmonary Hypertension," *Vascular Health and Risk Management* 2, no. 4 (2006): 411–422, doi:10.2147/vhrm.2006.2.4.411.

David Stipp, Robert Whitaker and Alicia Hills Moore, "The Selling of Impotence," *Fortune,* March 16, 1998.

Meika Loe. *The Rise of Viagra: How the Little Blue Pill Changed Sex in America* (New York: New York University Press, 2004), 31, 256.

Shereen El Feki, *Sex and the Citadel: Intimate Life in a Changing Arab World* (New York: Anchor Books, 2013), 75.

Geraldine Sealey, "Erections Get Insurance; Why Not the Pill?," *ABC News,* June 19, 2002.

Jane Weaver, "Wrigley Patents Anti-Impotence Gum," *NBC News,* accessed September 13, 2018.

Chris Wild, "Prehistoric Sex Toys," *Mashable,* January 13, 2015.

Hallie Lieberman, "How One of America's Greatest Ventriloquists Pioneered Female-Friendly Sex Toys," *Quartz,* December 21, 2017.

"Alabama Sex Toy Drive-Thru Business on the Rise," *Associated Press,* December 30, 2010.

SCIENCE

James Tozer, "Why Lawn Mowing is Better than Sex," *1843 Magazine,* March 2017.

Sharon Begley, "Claims of Virgin Births in US Near 1 Percent: Study," *Reuters,* December 17, 2013.

Taylor Kubota, "12 Things Every Man Should Know About His Balls," *Men's Journal,* December 1, 2014.

Mandy Mark, *In Your Face: 9 Sexual Studies* (New York: New York University Press, 2000), 98.

Stephanie Rosenbloom, "Pumpkin Pie: Provocative or Just Tasty?," *New York Times,* July 13, 2011.

Suzannah Weiss, "9 Fascinating Facts About Female Sexual Anatomy," *Bustle,* July 9, 2018.

Katherine Ellen Foley, "How Can a Set of Twins Have Completely different fathers?," *Quartz,* March 9, 2016.

Lawrence Altman, "Three Americans Awarded Nobel for Discoveries of How a Gas Affects the Body," *New York Times,* October 13, 1998.

Pamela Regan and Ellen Berscheid, *Lust: What We Know About Human Sexual Desire* (London: Sage Publications, Inc., 1999), 3.

Billi Gordon, "Well Hung," *Psychology Today,* February 27, 2014.

Aaron Ben-Zeev, "Why Did Descartes Love Cross-Eyed Women? The Lure of Imperfection," *Psychology Today,* November 29, 2011.

Dennis Overbye, "Einstein, Confused in Love and, Sometimes, Physics," *New York Times,* August 31, 1999.

Donald MacLeod, "Ancient Greeks Balls It Up," *The Guardian,* March 17, 2005.

Jeremy Laurence, "It's a Boy! The Science of Gender Selection," *The Independent,* April 24, 2008.

Andy Coghlan, "Darwin Dynasty's Ill Health Blamed on Inbreeding," *New Scientist,* May 3, 2010.

Jesse Bering, "Five Sex Research Pioneers You've Probably Never Heard Of," *Discover Magazine,* October 23, 2013.

Richard Rhodes, "Father of the Sexual Revolution," *New York Times,* November 2, 1997.

Hank Hyena, "Research Says Erect Gay Penises Are Bigger," *Salon,* November 4, 1999.

Mark Regnerus, *Forbidden Fruit: Sex & Religion in the Lives of American Teenagers* (Oxford: Oxford University Press, 2007), 4.

Melanie Tannenbaum, "Fear and Love on a Shaky Bridge," *Scientific American,* February 14, 2014.

Emily Shiffer, "Can an Orgasm Really Cure Your Cold?," *Men's Health,* December 6, 2017.

Michael Finkel, "While We Sleep, Our Mind Goes on an Amazing Journey," *National Geographic,* August 2018.

Helen Epstein, "God and the Fight Against AIDS," *The New York Review of Books,* April 28, 2005.

Maggie Koerth-Baker, "Space Sex Is Serious Business," *Five-ThirtyEight*, March 14, 2017.

A. J. Jacobs, "Space Oddities," *Boing Boing*, May 20, 2010.

Rae Paoletta, "Why NASA Just Sent Human Sperm on a SpaceX Rocket," *Inverse*, April 5, 2018.

Laura Poppick, "The Long, Winding Tale of Sperm Science," *Smithsonian*, June 7, 2017.

Seppo Kuukasjärvi et al., "Attractiveness of Women's Body Odors Over the Menstrual Cycle: The Role of Oral Contraceptives and Receiver Sex," *Behavioral Ecology* 15, no. 4 (2004): 579–584, doi:10.1093/beheco/arh050.

Steven Gangestad, Randy Thornhill, and Christine Garver-Apgar, "Women's Sexual Interests across the Ovulatory Cycle Depend on Primary Partner Developmental Instability," *Proceedings of the Royal Society of London B*: Biological Sciences 272, no. 1576 (2005): 2023–2027, doi: 10.1098/rspb.2005.3112.

Kristina Durante, Norman Li, and Martie Haselton, "Changes in Women's Choice of Dress across the Ovulatory Cycle: Naturalistic and Laboratory Task-Based Evidence," *Personality and Social Psychology Bulletin* 34, no. 11 (2008): 1451–1460, doi:10.1177/0146167208323103.

Nicolas Guéguen, "Makeup and Menstrual Cycle: Near Ovulation, Women Use More Cosmetics," *Psychological Record*, 62, no. 3 (2012): 541–548.

Martie Haselton et al., "Ovulatory Shifts in Human Female Ornamentation: Near Ovulation, Women Dress to Impress," *Hormones and Behavior*, 51, no. 1 (2007): 40–45, doi:10.1016/j.yhbeh.2006.07.007.

Alice Robb, "Unhappy Marriages May Produce More Daughters," *New Republic*, July 18, 2014.

Jesse Bering, "Not So Fast . . . What's So 'Premature' About Premature Ejaculation?," *Scientific American*, November 15, 2010.

Jean Stengers and Anne Van Neck, *Masturbation: The History of a Great Terror*, trans. Kathryn Hoffman (New York: St Martin's Press, 2001), 87.

David Buss, *The Dangerous Passion: Why Jealousy Is as Necessary as Love and Sex* (New York: Simon & Schuster, 2000), 57–60.

Justin Garcia et al., (2010). "Associations Between Dopamine D4 Receptor Gene Variation with Both Infidelity and Sexual Promiscuity," *PLoS One* 5, no. 11 (2010), doi:10.1371/journal.pone.0014162.

Leonard Derogatis and Katherine King. "The Coital Coronary: A Reassessment of the Concept." *Archives of Sexual Behavior* 10, no. 4 (1981): 325–335, doi:10.1007/BF01565536.

Reuben Fischer-Baum, "What's More Improbable: The Jaguars' +28 Line or an 11-Inch Penis?," *Deadspin*, October 7, 2013.

Christopher Riley, "The Dolphin Who Loved Me: The NASA-Funded Project That Went Wrong," *The Guardian*, June 8, 2014.

STDS

Agata Blaszczak-Boxe, "Pubic Hair Grooming May Raise STI Risk," *Live Science*, December 5, 2016.

"Why STDs are Soaring in America," *The Economist*, June 14, 2018.

Howard Markel, "The Real Story Behind Penicillin," *PBS Newshour*, September 27, 2013.

Mary Bowerman, "Antibiotic-Resistant Gonorrhea Is On the Rise: World Health Organization," *USA Today*, July 7, 2017.

Andrew Francis-Tan, "The Wages of Sin: How the Discovery of Penicillin Reshaped Modern Sexuality," *Archives of Sexual Behavior* 42, no. 1 (2013): 5–13, doi: 10.1007/s10508–012–0018–4.

"Male Circumcision for HIV Prevention," *World Health Organization*, accessed July 1, 2018.

Ed Vulliamy, "How Drug Giants Let Millions Die of AIDS," *The Observer*, December 18, 1999.

Abdullah Saeed, "Why a Community of Punks Chose to Infect Themselves with HIV in Castro's Cuba," *Vice*, February 1, 2017.

Kim Fredericks, "14 Facts About STDs That Could Save Your Life," *Reader's Digest*, July 12, 2018.

Alanna Greco, "5 Not-So-Fun Facts About Sexually Transmitted Diseases That You Probably Didn't Know," *Bustle*, January 23, 2014.

Tom Arvis, *Captain Condom and Lady Latex at War with the Army of Sex Diseases* (Washington DC: Program for Appropriate Technology in Health, 1991).

Peter Andreas, "Barriers to Entry," *Slate,* January 4, 2013.

Julia Naughton, "Wait, What?! Most Condoms on the Market Aren't Vegan," *Huffpost,* February 15, 2017.

Pamela Cryan and Chris Gaylord, "The 20 Most Fascinating Accidental Inventions," *CS Monitor,* October 5, 2012.

Fahd Khan et al., "The Story of the Condom," *Indian Journal of Urology* 29, no. 1 (2013): 12, doi:0.4103/0970–1591.109976.

Charles Goodyear, *The Applications and Uses of Vulcanized Gum-Elastic with Descriptions and Directions for Manufacturing Purposes Volume II* (New Haven, CT: Published for the Author, 1853), 9.

Tshireletso Motlogelwa, "PSI Pulls Out Controversial Condoms Adverts," *Mmegi Online,* May 10, 2007.

Roxanne Palmer, "A Brief History of the Condom," *Salon,* March 31, 2013.

"Condom Law Aftermath: Porn Production Booms in Las Vegas after Move from San Fernando Valley," *Associated Press,* January 17, 2014.

Data from Tubular Labs via email, accessed November 5, 2018.

"Largest Condom," Guinness World Records, accessed June 30, 2018.

"Largest Collection of Condoms," Guinness World Records, accessed June 30, 2018.

PORN

Tracy Clark-Flory, "What the Internet Reveals About Sexual Desire," *Salon*, May 2, 2011.

Patchen Barss, *The Erotic Engine: How Pornography Has Powered Mass Communication, from Gutenberg to Google* (Toronto: Anchor Canada, 2011).

Ashley Bowen, "5 Bits of Library of Congress Trivia for Its 217th Birthday!," *Book Riot*, April 24, 2017.

Walter Kendrick, *The Secret Museum: Pornography in Modern Culture* (Berkeley CA: University of California Press, 1987), 2.

Whitney Strub, "Why Libraries Need to Archive Porn," *Vice*, February 21, 2017.

Richard Nixon, "Special Message to the Congress on Obscene and Pornographic Materials," The American Presidency Project, accessed June 19, 2018.

Everett Holles, "Set Trial Goes to Jury on Coast," *New York Times*, December 19, 1971.

Karen Tumulty, "Prostitute's Claim Stuns Ministry to Runaways," *Los Angeles Times*, December 16, 1989.

Edwin McDowell, "Some Say Meese Report Rates an 'X,'" *New York Times*, October 21, 1986.

Linda Kauffman, *Bad Girls and Sick Boys: Fantasies in Contemporary Art and Culture* (Berkeley CA: University of California Press, 1998), 236.

Lester Haines, "Smoot—Can You Handle the Truth?," *The Register,* February 23, 2001.

Jennifer Bendery, "GOP Congresswoman Stands by Claim That Porn Leads to School Shootings," *Huffpost,* June 5, 2018.

Brian Merchant, "Whoever Has the Smallest Penis in Denmark Wins a New iPhone," *Motherboard,* October 12, 2012.

Kellen Beck, "The Often Gross and Rarely Sexy History of Video Game Sex," *Mashable,* August 15, 2018.

Steven Landsburg, "How the Web Prevents Rape," *Slate,* October 30, 2006.

Dan Ariely and George Loewenstein, "The Heat of the Moment: The Effect of Sexual Arousal on Sexual Decision Making," *Journal of Behavioral Decision Making* 19, no. 2 (2006): 87–98, doi:10.1002/bdm.501.

Seth Lubove, "See No Evil," *Forbes,* September 17, 2001.

Linda Greenhouse, "Supreme Court Roundup; Court Overrules Law Restricting Cable Sex Shows," *New York Times,* May 23, 2000.

Wall Turner, "Oregon Court Broadens Free Speech Rights," *New York Times,* April 15, 1987.

Stuart Taylor, "Court, 8–0, Extends Right to Criticize Those in Public Eye," *New York Times,* February 25, 1988.

"A Brief History of Film Censorship," National Coalition Against Censorship, accessed July 20, 2018.

"The Law: Home Movies," *Time*, April 18, 1969.

Eric Schlosser, *Reefer Madness: Sex, Drugs, and Cheap Labor in the American Black Market* (Boston: Houghton Mifflin Company, 2003), 202.

"Denmark: Pornography: What Is Permitted Is Boring," *Time*, June 6, 1969.

Jonathan Liew, "All Men Watch Porn, Scientists Find," *The Telegraph*, December 2, 2009.

Rachel Thompson, "Searches For Leprechaun Porn Predicted to Rise by 8,000% on St. Patrick's Day," *Mashable*, March 17, 2016.

Kaylin Pound, "Santa-Themed Porn Gets Really Popular Around Holidays," *Elite Daily*, December 22, 2016.

Zack Whittaker, "Civil Servant Who Watched Porn at Work Blamed for Infecting a US Government Network with Malware," *Tech Crunch*, October 29, 2018.

Dell Cameron, "DOJ's Amber Alert Website Is Redirecting Visitors to Hardcore Porn [Update: It's Worse Than We Thought]," *Gizmodo*, April 17, 2018.

Duncan Campbell, "Playboy Uncovered FBI Files Show Hoover Bought It for the Articles," *The Guardian*, October 9, 2000.

Aaron Smith, "Great Writers, Not Just Centerfolds, Have Filled the Pages of *Playboy*," CNN, September 28, 2017.

Jeremy Barr, "Playboy Hosting Its First White House Correspondents' Dinner Party," *Hollywood Reporter,* April 18, 2018.

Charles McGrath, "How Hef Got His Groove Back," *New York Times Magazine,* February 3, 2011.

Jim Puzzanghera, "Playboy Is Considering Ending Its Print Magazine, Report Says," *Los Angeles Times,* January 2, 2018.

POLITICS AND LAW

David Montero, "He May Be Dead, but Pimp Dennis Hof Wins Bid for Nevada State Assembly Seat," *Los Angeles Times,* November 7, 2018.

John Witte, *The Western Case for Monogamy over Polygamy* (New York: Cambridge University Press, 2015), 103.

"Egyptian Lawmakers: Ban Chinese Fake Hymen," *CBS News,* October 5, 2009.

Antonia Noori Farzan, "Georgia Mayor Plans to Round Up Sex Offenders on Halloween and House Them at City Hall," *Washington Post,* October, 24, 2018.

Elizabeth Weill-Greenberg, "When Handing out Candy to Trick-or-Treaters Means Risking Arrest," *The Appeal,* October 1, 2018.

Laura Bannister, "The Hard-On on Trial," *Paris Review,* May 18, 2016.

Mandy Caruso, "The X-Rated Furniture of Catherine the Great Is Something You Need to See," *BuzzFeed,* July 25, 2017.

Barbara Maranzani, "8 Things You Didn't Know About Catherine the Great," *History,* July 9, 2012.

Joseph Henrich, Robert Boyd, and Peter Richerson, "The Puzzle of Monogamous Marriage," *Philosophical Transactions of the Royal Society B*: Biological Sciences, 367, no. 1589 (2012): 657–669, doi:10.1098/rstb.2011.0290.

Lena Edlund et al., "More Men, More Crime: Evidence from China's One-Child Policy," *IZA Discussion Paper*, no. 3214, doi:10.1111/j.0042 –7092.2007.00700.x.

Andrea Tone, *Devices and Desires: A History of Contraceptives in America* (New York: Macmillan, 2002), 141–144.

Matthew Connelly, *Fatal Misconception: The Struggle to Control World Population* (Cambridge MA: Harvard University Press, 2009), 271.

Thomas Reese, "Vatican's Doctrinal Congregation Isn't So Supreme Anymore," *National Catholic Reporter,* February 14, 2014.

Jason Goldman, "What Can President Coolidge Teach Us About Sex?," *Gizmodo,* March 10, 2014.

Philip Sherwell, "The World According to Henry Kissinger," *The Telegraph,* May 21, 2011.

Larry Flynt and David Eisenbach, *One Nation under Sex: How the Private Lives of Presidents, First Ladies, and Their Lovers Changed the Course of American History* (New York: Macmillan, 2011), 22–25.

Jonathan Zimmerman, "Today's Politics Are Tame by 19th Century Standards," *Baltimore Sun,* August 13, 2015.

"The Long, Colorful History of the Mann Act," *NPR,* March 11, 2008.

Mark Small, "Involuntary Sterilization of Mentally Retarded Minors in Nebraska," *Nebraska Law Review* 68, no. 1 (1989): 410–429.

Cleve Wootson, "NBC Announced John McCain's Death—Then Abruptly Cut to Men Kissing in Dolphin Masks," *Washington Post,* August 26, 2018.

Jeet Heer, "The Presidential Penis: A Short History," *New Republic,* March 4, 2016.

John Carlin, "No Moles, No Growths, but Clinton Has His Blemishes," *The Independent,* November 15, 1997.

Eric Levenson, "President Warren Harding's Letters to His Mistress Were Hot and Heavy," *The Boston Globe,* July 8, 2014.

Tom McCarthy, "Stormy Daniels' Tell-All Book on Trump: Salacious Detail and Claims of Cheating," *The Guardian,* September 18, 2018.

Tierney McAfee, "Inside Trump's History with Playboy as It Preps to Make White House Correspondents' Dinner Debut," *People,* April 27, 2018.

Melina Delkic, "How Many Times Has Trump Cheated On His Wives? Here's What We Know," *Newsweek,* January 12, 2018.

Margaret Hartman, "What Happened to the 19 Women Who Accused Trump of Sexual Misconduct," *New York Magazine,* December 12, 2017.

Andrew Cohen, "There's a Gaping Hole in Giuliani and Trump's Legal Argument," *Rolling Stone*, May 3, 2018.

The Editorial Board, "The New Era of Abstinence," *New York Times*, May 5, 2018.

Paige Winfield Cunningham, "Trump Signs Anti-Pornography Pledge," *Washington Examiner*, August 1, 2016.

Christina Capatides, "Will Donald Trump Be the First President Who Has Been Divorced?," *CBS News*, November 9, 2016.

Mike Dash, "John Brinkley, The Goat-Gland Quack," *The Telegraph*, April 18, 2008.

Joseph Persico, *Franklin and Lucy: President Roosevelt, Mrs. Rutherfurd, and the Other Remarkable Women in His Life* (New York: Random House, 2008), 166.

Eyder Peralta, "Silenced Michigan State Rep To Perform 'Vagina Monologues' At State Capitol," *NPR*, June 17, 2012.

"2 Michigan Lawmakers Forced from Office over Affair Face Felony Charges," *Chicago Tribune*, February 26, 2016.

Andy Bloxham, "Allowing Women Drivers in Saudi Arabia Will Be 'End Of Virginity,'" *The Telegraph*, December 2, 2011.

Rosier Perper, "Saudi Arabia Makes History, Ending Longstanding Rule That Barred Women from Driving," *Business Insider*, June 24, 2018.

Dan Solomon, "Everything You Should Know About the Proposed Sex Robot Brothel in Houston," *Texas Monthly*, October 3, 2018.

Jim Loewen, "Our Real First Gay President," *Salon*, May 14, 2012.

Aaron Goldfarb, "When Presidents Talk Dirty: Statements Never Meant to Leave the White House," *MTV News*, October 1, 2014.

"Jackie Onassis Seduced Marlon Brando," *Page Six*, June 25, 2009.

Jack Holmes, "Yeah, This Congressional Race Features 'Bigfoot Erotica.' But Keep an Eye on the White Supremacy," *Esquire*, July 30, 2018.

John Noonan, *Contraception: A History of Its Treatment by the Catholic Theologians and Canonists* (Cambridge, MA: Harvard University Press, 1965), 21.

Piotr Scholz, *Eunuchs and Castrati: A Cultural History*, trans. Shelley Frisch and John Broadwin (Princeton NJ: Markus Wiener Publishers, 2001).

Malcolm Moore, "Away from the Desk: The World's Only Eunuch Museum," *The Telegraph*, October 18, 2002.

Vanessa Baird, *The No-Nonsense Guide to Sexual Diversity* (London: New Internationalist Publications Ltd, 2001), 122.

Philip Rucker and Dan Balz, "How Joni Ernst's Ad About 'Castrating Hogs' Transformed Iowa's US Senate Race," *Washington Post*, May 11, 2014.

Charlie Jane Anders, "A Map of the Weirdest Sex Laws in the United States," *io9*, December 17, 2013.

"Michigan Lawmakers Pushing to Overturn Cohabitation Law," *ABC 12*, February 28, 2018.

John Troyer, "Abuse of a Corpse: A Brief History and Re-Theorization of Necrophilia Laws in the USA." *Mortality* 13, no. 2 (2008): 132–152, doi:10.1080/13576270801954518.

ECONOMICS

Timothy Egan, "Erotica Inc.—A Special Report; Technology Sent Wall Street into Market for Pornography," *New York Times*, October 23, 2000.

"The Mainstream Corporations Profiting from Pornography," *Frontline*, February 2002.

Amin Ghaziani, *There Goes the Gayborhood?* (Princeton, NJ: Princeton University Press, 2014).

Jesse Walker, "Friday A/V Club: Donald Duck Explains Birth Control," *Reason*, March 20, 2015.

Katy Duke, "Project Retrains Prostitutes as Care Workers for Elderly People," *British Medical Journal* 332, no. 7542 (2006): 685, doi:10.1136/bmj.332.7543.685-a.

"Justices Reject Total Ban on 'Dial-a-Porn' Messages," *Associated Press*, June 25, 1989.

Frederick Lane, *Obscene Profits: Entrepreneurs of Pornography in the Cyber Age* (New York: Routledge, 2001), 157.

Anindya Sen and May Luong, "Estimating the Impact of Beer Prices on the Incidence of Sexually Transmitted Diseases: Cross-Province and Time Series Evidence From Canada," *Contemporary Economic Policy* 26, no. 4 (2008): 505–517, doi:10.1111/j.1465-7287.2008.00114.x.

Harrell Chesson, Paul Harrison, and William J. Kassler, "Sex Under the Influence: The Effect of Alcohol Policy on Sexually Transmitted Disease Rates in the United States," *The Journal of Law and Economics* 43, no. 1 (2000): 215–238, doi:10.1086/467453.

"Naked Capitalism," *The Economist,* September 26, 2015.

Jon Mooallem, "A Disciplined Business," *New York Times Magazine,* April 29, 2007.

Dino Grandoni, "Chart: Penile Length Leads to Little Economic Growth," *The Atlantic,* July 18, 2001.

Michele Boldrin, Mariacristina De Nardi, and Larry Jones, "Fertility and Social Security," *Journal of Demographic Economics* 81, no. 3 (2015): 261–299, doi:10.1017/dem.2014.14.

Jonathan Last, "Make Boomsa for the Motherland!," *Slate,* April 25, 2013.

Rachel Nuwer, "Singapore's 'National Night' Encourages Citizens to Make Babies," *Smithsonian,* August 8, 2012.

Vilhelm Carlström, "Is This Bizarre Ad Campaign Saving Denmark with Sex by Making Danes Have More Babies?," *Business Insider Nordic,* June 7, 2016.

Lily Katz, "Tulip Fever: There's a Digital Token for That, and So Much More," *Bloomberg,* September 8, 2017.

Sean O'Neal, "Insane Clown Posse Fans Now Have Their Own Digital Currency, the JuggaloCoin," *The A.V. Club,* April 14, 2014.

Khadeeja Safdar, "Under Armour's #MeToo Moment: No More Strip Clubs on Company Dime," *Wall Street Journal,* November 5, 2018.

Sarah Begley, "California Voters Reject Condom Requirement for Porn Industry," *Time,* November 9, 2016.

Mike McPhate, "California Today: Requiring the Use of Condoms in Adult Films," *New York Times,* October 4, 2016.

Mario Kato, "Abortion Still Key Birth Control," *Japan Times,* October 20, 2009.

Tiana Norgen, *Abortion Before Birth Control: The Politics of Reproduction in Postwar Japan* (Princeton, NJ: Princeton University Press, 2001), 82–88.

Adam Chandler, "Land of the Falling Son," *The Atlantic,* February 26, 2016.

"Population Ages 65 and Above (% of Total)," The World Bank, accessed June 21, 2018.

Roger Pulvers, "Reversing Japan's Rising Sex Aversion May Depend on a Rebirth of Hope," *Japan Times,* April 29, 2012.

Barbara Demick, "Judging China's One-Child Policy," *New Yorker,* October 30, 2015.

Mara Hvistendahl, *Unnatural Selection: Choosing Boys over Girls, and the Consequences of a World Full of Men* (New York: PublicAffairs, 2011), 185–192.

David Cox, "Hong Kong's Troubling Shortage of Men," *The Atlantic,* December 2, 2013.

Sushma Subramanian and Deborah Jian Lee, "For China's Educated Single Ladies, Finding Love Is Often a Struggle," *The Atlantic,* October 19, 2011.

Shang-Jin Wei and Xiaobo Zhang, "The Competitive Saving Motive: Evidence from Rising Sex Ratios and Savings Rates in China," *National Bureau of Economic Research*, no. 15093 (2009): doi:10.3386/w15093.

Bill Powell, "Gender Imbalance: How China's One-Child Law Backfired on Men," *Newsweek*, May 28, 2015.

MILITARY
"MI6 'Used Bodily Fluids as Invisible Ink,'" *The Telegraph*, September 21, 2010.

E. J. Dickson, "The Faulty Test Used to Punish Sex Offenders," *Vice*, June 7, 2016.

Angela Serratore, "The Curious Case of Nashville's Frail Sisterhood," *Smithsonian*, July 8, 2011.

John D'Emilio and Estelle Freedman, *Intimate Matters: A History of Sexuality in America* (Chicago: University of Chicago Press, 2012), 131.

Bill Jensen, "The Insane Story of the Guy Who Killed the Guy Who Killed Lincoln," *Washingtonian*, April 12, 2015.

Ann Landers, "Origins of 'Hooker' Hooks More than a Few Readers," *Chicago Tribune*, August 20, 1994.

Allan Brandt, *No Magic Bullet: A Social History of Venereal Disease in the United States Since 1880* (New York: Oxford University Press, 1987), 102.

Thomas Fleming, *The Illusion of Victory: America in World War I* (New York: Basic Books, 2004), 217.

Andrea Tone, *Devices and Desires: A History of Contraceptives in America* (New York: Macmillan, 2002), 98–110.

Lynne Haney and Lisa Pollard, eds., *Families of a New World: Gender, Politics, and State Development in a Global Context* (New York: Routledge, 2014), 50–52.

"Soldiers and Lovers: How Much the World's Armies Embrace Gays," *The Economist*, February 21, 2014.

Nathaniel Frank, *Unfriendly Fire: How the Gay Ban Undermines the Military and Weakens America* (New York: St. Martin's Press, 2009), 1.

Gary Lehring, *Officially Gay: The Political Construction of Sexuality* (Philadelphia: Temple University Press, 2010), 80–81.

Ben Brenkert, "Franklin D. Roosevelt's Forgotten Anti-Gay Sex Crusade," *The Daily Beast*, June 23, 2015.

"Homosexuals in Uniform," *Newsweek*, June 9, 1947.

Randy Shilts, *Conduct Unbecoming: Gays and Lesbians in the US Military* (New York: Macmillan, 1994), 66–67, 140.

"First Gay Rights Group in the US (1924)," *Chicago Tribune*, November 19, 2013.

Charles Kaiser, *The Gay Metropolis: The Landmark History of Gay Life in America* (New York: Grove Press, 1997), 51.

Amelia Abraham, "The Future of Our Gay Neighborhoods," *Vice*, September 18, 2014.

O'rene Daille Ashley, "The US Military Once Proposed a 'Gay' Bomb," *Gizmodo*, October 11, 2013.

Mary Roach, *Grunt: The Curious Science of Humans at War* (New York: W.W. Norton & Co., 2016), 15.

Michael Price, "Why We Think Monogamy Is Normal," *Psychology Today*, September 9, 2011.

John Witte, *The Western Case for Monogamy over Polygamy* (New York: Cambridge University Press, 2015), 108.

Tara John, "The Immortal Myth of Hitler's Deformed Genitals," *Time*, February 23, 2016.

"Genghis Khan, Warrior . . . and Sex God," *The Telegraph*, May 21, 2007.

Sara Nelson, "French Emperor Napoleon Bonaparte Had A 1.5 Inch Penis, Documentary Reveals," *Huffpost*, February 4, 2014.

"Art: Napoleon's Things," *Time*, February 14, 1927.

"The 'Dirt on Clean' in an Oversanitized World," *NPR*, November 17, 2007.

Charlotte Edwardes, "Historian Obsessed with Napoleon Spills the Beans on Bonaparte's Sex Life and Reveals the Truth About 'Not Tonight, Josephine,'" *Evening Standard*, June 10, 2015.

RELIGION

Piotr Scholz, *Eunuchs and Castrati: A Cultural History*, trans. Shelley Frisch and John Broadwin (Princeton NJ: Markus Wiener Publishers, 2001), 272–276.

Jean Wilson and Claus Roehrborn, "Long-Term Consequences of Castration in Men: Lessons From the Skoptzy and the Eunuchs of the Chinese and Ottoman Courts," *The Journal of Clinical Endocrinology & Metabolism* 84, no. 12 (1999): 4324–4331, doi:10.1210/jcem.84.12.6206.

Elizabeth Pisani, *The Wisdom of Whores: Bureaucrats, Brothels, and the Business of AIDS* (New York: W.W. Norton & Company, 2008), 201.

Dominic Janes, "The Confessional Unmasked: Religious Merchandise and Obscenity in Victorian England," *Victorian Literature and Culture 41*, no. 4 (2013): 677–690, doi:10.1017/S1060150313000168.

Ali Hamedani, "The Gay People Pushed to Change Their Gender," *BBC News*, November 5, 2014.

David Moye, "Montreal's Penis Temple Dedicated to Every Member (NSFW)," *Huffpost*, March 30, 2015.

"Aphrodisiac," Online Etymology Dictionary, accessed July 20, 2018.

"Hermaphrodite," Online Etymology Dictionary, accessed July 20, 2018.

"Priapism," Online Etymology Dictionary, accessed July 20, 2018.

Susan Schibanoff, *Chaucer's Queer Poetics: Rereading the Dream Trio* (Toronto: University of Toronto Press, 2006), 277.

Jon Blue, "The Case of the Piglet's Paternity," *Slate*, September 17, 2015.

Sofia Lotto Persio, "Festival of the Steel Phallus: Everything You Need to Know About Japan's Kanamara Matsuri," *Newsweek*, March 31, 2018.

Carrie Weisman, "A Brief History of Penis Worship," *AlterNet,* November 30, 2015.

"First Council of Nicaea (A.D. 325)," *New Advent,* accessed July 8, 2018.

Garry Wills, *The Future of the Catholic Church with Pope Francis* (New York: Viking, 2015), 71.

Havelock Ellis, *Studies in the Psychology of Sex: Sex in Relation to Society* (Philadelphia: F.A. Davis Company Publishers, 1911), 283.

John Noonan, *Contraception: A History of Its Treatment by the Catholic Theologians and Canonists* (Cambridge, MA: Harvard University Press, 1965), 35, 163.

James Brundage, *Law, Sex, and Christian Society in Medieval Europe* (Chicago: University of Chicago Press, 1987), 221.

Judy Thomas, "Catholic Priests Are Dying of AIDS, Often in Silence," *The Kansas City Star,* January 29, 2000.

Danny Hughes, David Mitchell, and David Molinari, "Heeding the Call: Seminary Enrollment and the Business Cycle," *Applied Economics Letters* 18 (2011): 433–437, doi:10.1080/13504851003689668.

T. W. Burger, "Enrollment at Seminaries Surges During Trying Times," *Patriot-News,* March 7, 2009.

Tom Roberts, "Bishops Were Warned of Abusive Priests," *National Catholic Reporter,* March 30, 2009.

Paul Vitello, "Prospective Catholic Priests Face Sexuality Hurdles," *New York Times,* May 30, 2010.

Malcolm Gladwell, "John Rock's Error," *New Yorker,* March 10, 2000.

Max Cortesi, "Chimi Lhakhang," *Atlas Obscura,* accessed August 9, 2018.

Tom Chivers, "11 Seriously Weird Facts About Jesus's Foreskin," *BuzzFeed,* November 5, 2015.

John Durant, *The Paleo Manifesto: Ancient Wisdom for Lifelong Health* (New York: Harmony, 2013), 60.

Travis Andrews, "One of the Shakers' Last Three Members Died Monday. The Storied Sect Is Verging on Extinction," *Washington Post,* January 4, 2017.

"Travel—Books in Brief," *The Times Literary Supplement,* May 15, 1998.

Marcia Inhorn and Soraya Tremayne, eds., "Islam, Assisted Reproduction, and the Bioethical Aftermath," *Journal of Religion and Health* 54, no. 6 (2015): 1–9, doi:10.1007/s10943–015–0151–1.

Zoe Williams, "IVF: 'Where's All That Grief Going?,'" *The Guardian,* September 27, 2013.

CULTURE

Pascale Harter, "Mauritania's 'Wife-Fattening' Farm," *BBC News,* January 26, 2004.

"Would You Be Beautiful in the Ancient World?," *BBC News,* January 10, 2015.

Kyung-Jim Min, Cheol-Koo Lee, and Han-Nam Park, "The Lifespan of Korean Eunuchs," *Current Biology* 22, no. 18 (2012): 792–793, doi:10.1016/j.cub.2012.06.036.

Lucas Reilly, "Mozart Wrote Dirty Songs, Too," *Mental Floss*, February 26, 2014.

"Robot Sex Poll Reveals Americans' Attitudes About Robotic Lovers, Servants, Soldiers," *Huffpost*, April 10, 2013.

Dan Levin, "Beach Essentials in China: Flip-Flops, a Towel and a Ski Mask," *New York Times*, August 3, 2012.

Evan Andrews, "10 Things You May Not Know About Roman Gladiators," *History*, March 4, 2014.

"Do They Work? 5 Popular Aphrodisiacs," *Time*, February 14, 2011.

Wiktionary, "Ithyphallophobia," accessed October 20, 2018.

Kristin Winet, "Rasputin Was Poisoned, Shot, Beaten, and Drowned. But Did His Penis Survive?," *Atlas Obscura*, June 24, 2015.

Thomas Hickman, *God's Doodle: The Life and Times of the Penis* (Berkeley CA: Soft Skull Press, 2013), 25.

John D'Emilio and Estelle Freedman, *Intimate Matters: A History of Sexuality in America* (Chicago: The University of Chicago Press, 1988), 190.

Elina Pradhan, "Female Education and Childbearing: A Closer Look at the Data," *The World Bank*, November 24, 2015.

Claire Cain Miller, "The Divorce Surge Is Over, but the Myth Lives On," *New York Times*, December 2, 2014.

Danielle Teller and Astro Teller, "The 50% Divorce Rate Stat Is a Myth, So Why Won't It Die?," *Quartz*, December 4, 2014.

Kyung Lah, "Divorce Ceremonies Give Japanese Couples a New Way to Untie the Knot," CNN, September 7, 2010.

Wendy Wang, "The Link Between a College Education and a Lasting Marriage," Pew Research Center, December 4, 2015.

A. J. Jacobs, *The Know-It-All: One Man's Humble Quest to Become the Smartest Person in the World* (New York: Simon & Schuster, 2004), 130.

Michael Castleman, "How Women Really Feel About Penis Size," *Psychology Today*, November 1, 2014.

Andrew Harding, "Beijing's Penis Emporium," *BBC News*, September 23, 2006.

Malcolm Moore, "Away from the Desk: The World's Only Eunuch Museum," *The Telegraph*, October 18, 2002.

Alex, "Orchiectomy—Removing the Testicles," *Vice*, March 12, 2010.

Frank Newport, "In US, Estimate of LGBT Population Rises to 4.5%," Gallup, May 22, 2018.

Garance Franke-Ruta, "Americans Have No Idea How Few Gay People There Are," *The Atlantic*, May 31, 2012.

Helen Fisher, *Anatomy of Love: A Natural History of Mating, Marriage, and Why We Stray* (New York: Random House, 1992), 42, 253.

"Median Age at First Marriage: 1890 to Present," US Census Bureau, Decennial Censuses, 1890 to 1940, and Current Population Survey,

Annual Social and Economic Supplements, 1947 to 2017, accessed August 1, 2018.

Jean Stengers and Anne Van Neck, *Masturbation: The History of a Great Terror*, trans. Kathryn Hoffman (New York: St Martin's Press, 2001), 2.

"8 Words From Nahuatl," Merriam-Webster, accessed August 2, 2018.

Piotr Scholz, *Eunuchs and Castrati: A Cultural History*, trans. Shelley Frisch and John Broadwin (Princeton NJ: Markus Wiener Publishers, 2001), 52.

Michael Schuman, "On an Indonesian Isle, Kidnapping Is the Way to Win a Woman's Heart," *Wall Street Journal*, May 29, 2001.

Elena Nicolaou, "The True Story Behind Mary Shelley Is Actual 19th Century Rock & Roll," *Refinery29*, May 24, 2018.

Stacy Conradt, "Mary Shelley's Favorite Keepsake: Her Dead Husband's Heart," *Mental Floss*, July 8, 2015.

Jacqueline Howard, "Fewer Teens Having Sex and Using Drugs, CDC Survey Finds," CNN, June 14, 2018.

Amanda MacMillan, "Teens Today Are Having Sex, Dating and Drinking Less Than They Used To," *Time*, September 19, 2017.

John Witte, "Why Two in One Flesh? The Western Case for Monogamy over Polygamy," *Emory Law Journal* 64 (2014): 1675–1746.

Patrick Gray, "Ethnographic Atlas Codebook," *World Cultures* 10, no. 1 (1998): 86–136.

David Blanchflower and Andrew Oswald, "Money, Sex and Happiness: An Empirical Study," *National Bureau of Economic Research*, no. 10499 (2004): 393–415, doi:10.3386/w10499.

Richard Conniff, "Go Ahead, Kiss Your Cousin," *Discover Magazine*, August 1, 2003.

Mona Chalabi, "How Many Americans Are Married to Their Cousins?," *FiveThirtyEight*, May 15, 2015.

Matt Stopera, "FYI, You Can Still Marry Your Cousin in North Carolina," *BuzzFeed*, May 9, 2012.

Neel Burton, "My Hero Diogenes the Cynic," *Psychology Today*, March 11, 2012.

Iva Roze Skoch, "Welcome to Thailand: The Penis Shrine," Public Radio International, February 9, 2012.

Bel Mooney, "The Madness of Offering the Mentally Disabled Sex With Prostitutes At Taxpayers' Expense," *Daily Mail*, August 18, 2010.

Vern Bullough and James Brundage, eds., *Handbook Of Medieval Sexuality* (New York: Routledge, 1996), 134.

Bradley Jolly, "Woman Sues Ex-Boyfriend after His 'Abnormally Long' Penis 'Stretched Her Vagina,'" *Daily Mirror*, November 9, 2018.

Ryan Jacobs, "The Strange Sexual Quirk of Filipino Seafarers," *The Atlantic*, August 9, 2013.

Natasha Hinde, "Woman Makes Sourdough Using Yeast from Vagina, Sends Twitter Into Meltdown," *Huffpost*, November 24, 2015.

Tom Adams, "Leicester City's Premier League Title Win: The Greatest Underdog Story Of All," *Eurosport,* March 5, 2016.

Kelly-Ann Mills, "Man Whose Genitals Were Bitten Off by Bulldog 'Had Smeared Himself with Peanut Butter,'" *Daily Mirror,* November 2, 2018.

Alexandra Sifferlin, "Environmentalist Hugs a Tree by Marrying It," *Time,* November 24, 2014.

Chip Brown, "The Many Ways Society Makes a Man," *National Geographic,* January 2017.

Mary Roach, *Bonk: The Curious Coupling of Science and Sex* (New York: W.W. Norton & Co., 2008), 132.

Daniel Boffey, "Dutch Man, 69, Starts Legal Fight to Identify as 20 Years Younger," *The Guardian,* November 8, 2018.

Chris Yuscavage, "Hulk Hogan Asked to Answer Awkward Questions About the Size of His Penis During Sex Tape Trial," *Complex,* March 8, 2016.

Jessica Wapner, "The Troubled History of the Foreskin," *Mosaic,* February 24, 2015.